PIECE
BY
PIECE™

PIECE
BY
PIECE™

A

COMMONSENSE

APPROACH

TO A

SECURE

RETIREMENT

DEBBIE CRAIG
CFP®, MBA, CRPS®

Published by Advantage, Charleston, South Carolina.
Member of Advantage Media Group.

ADVANTAGE is a registered trademark, and the Advantage colophon is a trademark of Advantage Media Group, Inc.

Certified Financial Planner Board of Standards Inc. owns the certification marks CFP®, Certified Financial Planner™ and federally registered CFP (with flame design) in the U.S., which it awards to individuals who successfully complete CFP Board's initial and ongoing certification requirements.

Printed in the United States of America.

ISBN: 978-1-59932-734-1
LCCN: 2016939734

This publication is designed to provide accurate and authoritative information in regard to the subject matter covered. It is sold with the understanding that the publisher is not engaged in rendering legal, accounting, or other professional services. If legal advice or other expert assistance is required, the services of a competent professional person should be sought.

Advantage Media Group is proud to be a part of the Tree Neutral® program. Tree Neutral offsets the number of trees consumed in the production and printing of this book by taking proactive steps such as planting trees in direct proportion to the number of trees used to print books. To learn more about Tree Neutral, please visit **www.treeneutral.com.** To learn more about Advantage's commitment to being a responsible steward of the environment, please visit **www.advantagefamily.com/green.**

Advantage Media Group is a publisher of business, self-improvement, and professional development books and online learning. We help entrepreneurs, business leaders, and professionals share their Stories, Passion, and Knowledge to help others Learn & Grow. Do you have a manuscript or book idea that you would like us to consider for publishing? Please visit **advantagefamily.com** or call **1.866.775.1696.**

To Neal and Chris~
For your love along life's journey.

TABLE OF CONTENTS

ACKNOWLEDGMENTS

I f it takes a village to raise a child, it must take the entire province to produce a book. There are so many people to thank for the pages I'm holding now.

I would not have written this book if I didn't have so many wonderful clients. They'd seem to appear in my practice just when I needed them to challenge me on a new investment concept. When we experienced the "dot-com" or "dot-bomb" era in 2000–2002, I so appreciated my clients' steadfastness. They would question things, but ultimately they wanted to do what would be best over the long term for their portfolio. The trust that I have experienced from them through the years is humbling. As I relate in chapter 2, one client who was taking required minimum distributions from his account really started my thinking on a new way to manage accounts for retirement income. Thanks to him for unabashedly raising so many good questions, which generated my thoughts and became the foundation for the Piece by Piece™ model.

Over the years, I have had some excellent teachers and professors. With regard to this book, I want to specifically point out Rosalie Allen, my high-school English teacher. I thought I was a pretty good writer before entering her class, but she definitely zeroed in on some rough edges. Every paper came back with the margins filled with "ww" for "wrong word" and "awk" for "awkward sentence structure." Kudos to her for not just letting me slide by but challenging me to become a better writer.

I used my Thanksgiving holiday vacation to start on this publishing process. I appreciate my family for putting up with my mental absence. They understand the passion I have to be an awesome financial advisor (Does the one with the most continuing ed credits win?) and to get an item (writing a book) off my bucket list. It all takes a lot of time and energy away from them. They never complain about basic meals (cereal for dinner) or when I get called away by a phone call or closet myself behind a closed door. I'm grateful for their presence in my life and the way they have enriched my life's journey.

Finally, thank you to my amazing publishing team at Advantage Media. To my project editor, Mary Berry, who had to put up with my calls when she was moving. To Scott, Lindsey, Adam, Brette, Allison, Kirk, Nate, Matthew, and a host of others who brought this whole crazy project of mine to fruition. Thank you all.

INTRODUCTION
RETIRE WITH CONFIDENCE!

My Grandmother worked for herself, as a hair stylist in a salon. Every time she needed a little extra cash, she would go to the refrigerator, open up the vegetable crisper, unroll a piece of foil, and take out a $20 bill. We always called it "Nanny's cold cash." This stash also may have been the extent of her retirement planning, other than her Social Security check every month.

In the Detroit neighborhood where I grew up in the seventies, it seemed like everyone else's parents were set for life with pensions from their jobs with the Big Three motor corporations. My Dad, though, was a small business owner—an independent insurance adjuster, with four branches in Michigan—so he did not have a pension to look forward to. I was always well aware that there was not going to be anybody waiting with a check for him every month at the other end of his career.

Helping people like my parents to retire with confidence, and have a monthly check for the rest of their lives without having to raid the fridge has always been a concern for me.

It turns out that my Dad and my Grandmother were ahead of their time. According to the Small Business Administration, more than 99 percent of workers in the United States work for businesses with fewer than five hundred employees. Today, 50 percent of working Americans have no pension or defined-benefits plan. Defined-benefit

1

plans continue to dwindle, becoming exception rather than rule. As of 2011, only 10 percent of private employers offered pension plans, accounting for 18 percent of the private workforce.[1] People who were hired at General Motors after 1993 have no pension plan, for example, and even the biggest corporations in America have no pension plans anymore. In general, the only people with pensions today are governmental employees, teachers, and municipal workers, such as those at police and fire departments. And even this situation is changing.

Companies big and small may put matching funds (often 4 percent) into a 401(k) or a retirement plan for their employees, which these employees take with them when they leave. It's also becoming the norm for employees of companies both large and small to put additional money away for their own retirement.

In other words, most of us working Americans now have to save the money for our retirement on our own. We aim to get to the end of working life with—we hope—a nest egg. But how do we use this money to create a "pension" for ourselves for the rest of our lives? How can we feel sure that our nest egg will last as long as we do?

Even those who don't work for others—small business owners— need to be thinking about a personal retirement plan. Many small business owners invest in their companies with the idea that their business is their retirement plan. They think, *When I get ready to retire, I'll just sell the company, and that money will become my nest egg.* That is not a commonsense approach, because a lot of things can happen. Number one, you can't force somebody to buy your company when you need to sell it; the timing could easily be off.

---

1 William J. Wiatrowski, "The Last Private Industry Pension Plans: A Visual Essay," *Monthly Labor Review* (December 2012): 3–1, http://www.bls.gov/opub/mlr/2012/12/ art1full.pdf.

Number two, many times you *are* your company, and when you're not there anymore, there is no company.

When I work with small business owners, I suggest creating a framework that can be used later on—just in case. If you are able to sell your business and make a million dollars, it's a bonus. But just in case your business does not sell, you will have a plan in place to potentially live on. The same kind of plan that I create for individuals who are getting ready to retire can be put in place early on for a small business owner.

MY GOAL: YOUR FINANCIAL SECURITY

Back in 2000, I began seeing a need for an understandable, commonsense approach to retirement security. At the time, I was working with many people within five or ten years of retirement who had nest eggs but were nervous about what to do in the face of a very volatile financial market. Back in the old days, we did not have to worry so much about the market going up and down. People were more likely to have a pension to live on, so what was in the market was "just" their investments for their extra money. However, that was not going to be the case going forward. We were going to have to take care of ourselves.

To help these people prepare for retirement, I made it a goal to discover a way to utilize this money in a less-risky approach so that these clients would not run out of their nest egg, no matter how long they lived. Essentially, they needed a plan they could feel confident in so that they could take the next step into retirement. Though it sounds like the easiest thing in the world to many people, actually taking that step and retiring can be difficult. Not only are you no longer contributing to your retirement account; you are also starting to draw from it—it's a double whammy. If you have been a saver and have always contributed 10 percent from your paycheck into a savings account, it can be psychologically and emotionally tough to start pulling 5 percent out of your accounts every year and using it to live on. In fact, some people cannot do it. One of my clients wanted to go back to work after about a year because she was used to seeing the balances go up; she could not handle seeing them come down.

To help feel more secure in your retirement, you should consider developing a relationship with a financial planner you really trust. After all, you are having a conversation about how to use money that you have worked for your entire life; you are determining the kinds of things you want to have happen in the next thirty or even forty years or more. After all, if you're lucky, you will be in retirement for as long as you were working.

With that in mind, you can't settle for someone who just says, "Trust me, it's all going to work out." I believe you should consider working with someone who has a commonsense approach to help generate that income check and utilize your savings—and who is also willing to take time to explain it to you in a way you can understand. It is not enough for a financial planner to tell you about a plan, pat you on the head, and say, "Trust me." You deserve confidence in your retirement years.

Recently, I struck up a conversation with a stranger on a flight. When I told him I'm a financial advisor, he said, "I'm going to go meet with my financial advisor tomorrow, but you know, everything he says goes over my head." I was speechless for a minute. If your advisor is always talking over your head I believe that is probably not the advisor for you. Find someone willing to spend time with you and explain your plan as thoroughly as necessary. You will feel more confident if you understand what is going on, I believe you will feel more confident that you may not have to move in with your kids or become a greeter at Walmart.

To address these concerns, I created a retirement-income plan called *Piece by Piece*™, designed for anyone moving from their earning years into their retirement years. I wanted to help my clients to create a lifetime stream of income from their nest egg that replaces wages from employment, no matter what the market is doing. I've had the good fortune—or bad luck, depending on how you look at it—to test my plan during the very difficult financial times that have occurred since 2000.

Piece by Piece™ divides your nest egg—which is a combination of your investments, rollovers, pensions, Social Security, and annuities—into three pieces, each with a distinct goal: (1) *Income Today*, a portion designed to create the income you'll require every month in your retirement years; (2) *Income Tomorrow*, a portion designed to create increased income that might be needed due to inflation, health care, or other special needs; and (3) *Flexibility Dollars*, a portion for unforeseen things. Some things just cannot be planned for, but we can still have provisions for them.

Keep in mind that there is not assurance that any strategy will ultimately be successful or profitable nor protect against a loss.

The sensationalism on the twenty-four-hour news channels will never stop—but you should be confident knowing that you have a plan in place designed to always generate income through volatile markets.

HOW IS PIECE BY PIECE™ DIFFERENT?

Now, I'm not saying that other methods of retirement-income planning are completely without merit. There are three largely accepted methods for managing retirement-income distributions: the *bucket approach*, the *systematic-withdrawal approach*, and the *necessities-versus-luxuries approach*. According to a research study called "Financial Advisor Retirement Income Planning Experiences, Strategies, and Recommendations," conducted by the Financial Planning Association (FPA), advisors use the systematic-withdrawal approach 53.9 percent of the time, while the bucket strategy is used 29.4 percent of the time. The third approach—necessities-versus-luxuries—is utilized by approximately 26.2 percent of financial planners.

Years 1-3   Years 4-12   Years 13-25

The bucket approach is a commonly used planning model that is easy to visualize as separate "buckets" of investments based on the time horizon for requiring income. The approach sets aside money in three portions: one bucket for money you will use in one to three years, a second bucket for money you will use in four to twelve years, and the third bucket for money you will use further in your retirement years. Investments in the funds in each bucket have different risk approaches, and you sell some out of each bucket and move money through the different buckets.

Cash and cash alternatives or short-term investments would fill the first bucket. The idea is that there will be less volatility or loss of principle in these investments. Money will be available when the retiree needs it.

Bucket two would have investments with a mid-term risk profile. The investments would be subjected to some market volatility because the retiree wouldn't need the income in the shorter term and should allow the investments to recover from downdrafts in value. Intermediate bonds and dividend-paying stocks (like utilities) would be included in the middle bucket.

Bucket three would include growth stocks. Because of the longer time horizon before needing the money, these investments would sustain market movement over longer periods of time. Stocks without dividends, international holdings, emerging market stocks, commodities, and longer-term bonds would all be included.

This approach may intuitively appeal to investors, since the first two or three years of "retirement checks" are secured as cash. Investors can feel more confident to know that the everyday market movements can be ignored, since there is cash available designed to meet their daily needs. However, I am uncomfortable with this approach because of the somewhat arbitrary ways that money needs to move between buckets. When do I move money from bucket to bucket? Should I "peel off" profit from bucket two when the market is up? Should dividends and interest from bucket two be moved when they are earned? Or should a certain percentage of money be moved on a regular basis (quarterly or annually) regardless of market performance? Having been an advisor during the 2000–2002 bear market, I know that these decisions are not easy ones. If a client retired on January 1, 2000 and had cash in bucket 1 for 2000, 2001, and 2002, it is likely that the investments in buckets two and three would have fallen significantly in value. Selling in this market may have made liquidating into the cash bucket (bucket one) painful, as the sale of the reduced value of investments may have locked in the retiree's losses. Essentially, you would have to sell something when it's down in the five-year bucket to fill the three-year bucket. I believe a more predictable, stable approach to investing for your retirement should include an agreement between the advisor and the client, which would automatically refill the cash bucket, similar to the "Income Today" approach of dividends and interest.

The second retirement-income strategy—the systematic-withdrawal approach—is based on the assumption that there is a "safe withdrawal rate"—typically around 4 percent. The advisor and client discuss an investment policy with specific stocks, bonds, mutual funds, and/or separately managed accounts. The retiree then draws the agreed-to percentage (say 4 percent) from the total portfolio. There is still some flexibility in this approach, as some advisors adjust upward each year for inflation. Clients who are more risk-averse would still take the recommended withdrawal percentage but might have more dividend-paying stocks and bonds—while an aggressive investor may choose to have a portfolio of mostly growth, international, and emerging market stocks and low-quality bonds.

Another way is to pull an even amount from every investment you own, but I always wonder how you would know whether you might be pulling out an investment that might recover and be more valuable later on. I am also uncomfortable with this: Imagine that I'm a chicken farmer who keeps selling off 4 percent of my hens each year. If I do that year after year, how am I going to have any hens producing eggs toward the end of my retirement? What *does* make sense to me is to generate income from my hens in the form of eggs that I could potentially live on. In that way, I may not have to worry so much about selling off the hens—because I know that they should continue to lay those eggs.

The third approach—necessities-versus-luxuries—requires the client to set a budget for necessities (rent, food, utilities, insurance, healthcare costs, clothing, etc.) and then fund these items with guaranteed income streams like pensions and Social Security. This need could also be met with an immediate annuity for a client without a pension. This planning approach sets a "floor" of income, which meets a client's necessities budget. Luxuries are funded with the remainder of the client's portfolio and invested in nonguaranteed or growth-oriented investments (such as stocks). In a down market, the client would be unable to make any withdrawals in order to fund their luxuries. Depending on the client's situation, this might include not traveling to a grandchild's destination wedding or replacing their shag carpeting.

Above all, it is also important to me that the plan be based on a client's personality and individual needs and wishes. If you were a coupon clipper when you were working, you will probably be a coupon clipper in retirement. If you traveled a lot, you probably won't want to stop traveling once you retire. If you want to leave a legacy, or if you want to spend most of your money in the first five years because you have a chronic health condition that will progress, we can help figure it out.

That is the best part of Piece by Piece™—it's customizable for your situation but doesn't force you to make difficult choices in bad (or good) markets. Instead, Piece by Piece™ is designed to strategically divide your nest egg into three pieces to help provide Income Today, Income Tomorrow, and Flexibility Dollars.

Whether you are nearing retirement or you have decades to go, this book will teach you how Piece by Piece™ is designed to:

1. Create the income you'll require every month in retirement.

2. Create increased income that might be needed in the future due to inflation, health care, or other special needs.

3. Plan for unforeseen events.

Above all, I want my clients to be more confident in retirement because we have a plan, we are working that plan, and it is working for them. Retirement time is best spent investing in new passions— hobbies, travel, family. That's the goal, and we'll work on it together, every step of the way. No one should have to worry about how much cash is left in the veggie crisper!

Keep in mind that there is not assurance that any strategy will ultimately be successful or profitable nor protect against a loss.

CHAPTER 1

YOUR PRECIOUS NEST EGG

Until recently, we could count on three sources for our retirement income: a pension, Social Security, and our savings. Today, if you have a pension, you're one of the lucky few. Most people now must rely on their Social Security payments and their nest egg—their savings, often a 401(k) plan or Roth IRA—once they retire and then for the rest of their lives. Many of us are worried about running out of money in retirement, afraid that we'll have to go back to work at a low-paying job or become a burden to our children.

If you are within five to ten years of retirement, I believe it's time to put your nest egg to work. Even as you are still adding to your retirement savings, it's important to have a plan to help ensure that when it comes time to utilize that money, it may help you to retire with an income plan. And even if you are closer to retiring, careful financial planning is still invaluable.

MY AH-HA MOMENT: THE NEED FOR A NEW METHOD TO HELP ENSURE CONFIDENCE IN RETIREMENT

It was 2002—the market was down 50 percent from its high in the dot-com era just two years earlier. A seventy-three-year-old physician came to me for a second opinion on his retirement plan, which someone else had set up for him. Since he'd turned seventy and one-half, he'd had to take distributions (called RMDs for required minimum distributions) from his IRAs based on the market's performance on December 31 of the prior year. The market was down 25 percent from that time, but he still had to take out the required money. There was no waiting until the market went back up.

The physician asked, "When am I going to get my money back and my nest egg built up again?" And I had to reply, "Never." He was stunned and didn't know how to respond. I'm pretty sure that he'd been told (and believed) that the market would recover (which it did). He'd been sure that his account value would pop back up with the market—though individual security values might not.

Market prices would go up eventually, of course, but he would not have the shares to ride that appreciation back up—because he had been forced to sell more shares as the market was going down. He might have had to sell two shares last year, but this year, due to price depreciation, he would have to sell three shares to get the same amount of money.

As an example*:

If his RMD for last year was $12,000 and the share price was $10, he would have to liquidate 1,200 shares.

$$10/12,000=1,200$$

This year the share price is $7.50 (a decrease of 25 percent), so his RMD of $12,000 would necessitate selling 1,600 shares.

$$7.5/12,000=1,600$$

The client would own four hundred fewer shares to appreciate in value with a market recovery.

And the IRS specified how much money he had to take out. He needed an income-generating investment to cover his RMDs so that the growth portion of his portfolio would have time to recover. Happily, this is how we chose to reconfigure his portfolio.

As we were chatting in my office, a lightbulb went on in my head: We needed a method to help people avoid this situation. We needed a framework that would utilize that nest egg without selling off the hens. It would eventually take many weeks and iterations to develop this framework. Back in the old days, when people had a pension, they did not have to worry about the market going up and down. Their investments often were just gravy above and beyond their pension. That was not going to be the case going forward. We were going to have to take care of ourselves—be responsible for our own retirement planning.

---

*This is a hypothetical illustration and is not intended to reflect the actual performance of any particular security. Future performance cannot be guaranteed and individual investor's results will vary.

I wanted a commonsense approach to help people utilize their nest egg—their portfolio—to create what amounted to a "pension" check for themselves. And I wanted to have a way to do it that made more sense than merely hoping and praying that the market goes up and then selling off the profit. That might have worked during the earlier dot-com years, when the market soared, but it was not going to work going forward, and it sure wasn't working in 2002. I wanted to figure out a method designed to help my clients generate an income stream in retirement that might always be there, regardless of interest rates and regardless of what the stock market or the bond market was doing.

In short, I wanted to be able to ensure my clients—who are my friends and neighbors in this small town—that they can retire with confidence. That is what I started doing more than fifteen years ago—and it seems I chose a fifteen-year period when the economy has been particularly challenging. People are living longer and having to rely on themselves more for making their money last. But that is only part of the challenge. The twenty-first century so far has been a precarious time for people to retire. The year 2000 ushered in the dot-com (or dot-bomb) era for stocks, and the market has not given them the returns that they had hoped for and needed. Also, the bond market has not been a good place to wait it out. Interest rates have been abysmally low—since 2008, interest rates (and their reflection in bond interest) have been lower than in decades. The Piece by Piece™ plan has been reality tested with volatile stock prices and low bond rates.

Every investor's situation is unique and you should consider your investment goals, risk tolerance and time horizon before making any investment. Keep in mind that there is no assurance that any strategy will ultimately be successful or profitable nor protect against a loss.

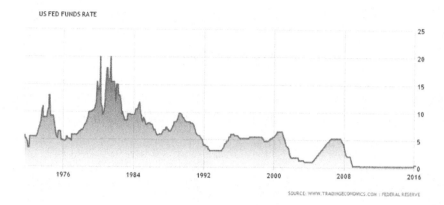

US FED FUNDS RATE

This graph indicates the US Federal Funds Rate from 1971 to 2016. The highest rate was recorded in March 1980 at 20 percent, and the lowest rate recorded was in December 2008 at 0.25 percent. Over the forty-five-year time frame, the rate has averaged 5.9 percent. The current rate can be viewed on the US Treasury website at www.treasury.gov.

RETIREMENT INCOME TODAY

Twenty years ago in retirement-income planning, we would talk about a three-legged stool: your pension, your Social Security, and your savings made up approximately equal parts of your retirement income. And, once again, most people no longer have pensions, so most of us have to rely on Social Security and savings.

Social Security was never meant to take the place of pensions or take care of all our financial needs. Many people believe that since they have put a lot into Social Security, they will get a commensurable amount back. This may not always be true. For a person who makes $50,000 a year, Social Security benefits will replace only 50 percent of that preretirement income. For someone used to making $100,000 a year, Social Security will replace only 25 percent of that income. People at both income levels still need to fill in the gaps once they retire.

PENSIONS

A pension is typically called a *defined-benefit* plan, in which an employer makes contributions on behalf of an employee and guarantees a specific benefit at a certain retirement age. The employer is responsible for making sure that the investment performance is adequate to provide for the benefit at retirement.

These plans have mostly been replaced by defined-contribution plans within private industry. The employer generally deposits a percentage of an employee's compensation. The employee is also able to make contributions to this same retirement account (to a limit defined in the law). There is no guarantee of a specific benefit at retirement. The employee is generally responsible for investing these funds within plan investments chosen by the employer. This change has made employees generally responsible for managing their own retirement nest egg accumulation. Investment performance and "risk" of having enough has been shifted to the individual.

To the extent that pensions still exist, they are generally available for education and government workers only. According to the latest information from the Bureau of Labor Statistics (BLS), in 2011, 10 percent of all private-sector employers provided a pension plan to retirees. During the same year, 78 percent of public-sector employees benefitted from a pension. Unfortunately, the percentage of employees in all sectors covered by a pension continue to drop, forcing retirees to depend more on themselves and their savings.

Definition	Lowest	2nd	3rd	4th	Highest
Final earnings	137	77	69	52	42
PV payment	62	47	42	40	36
Wage-indexed average earnings	70	52	45	41	36
CPI average	82	60	53	48	42

Authors' calculations based on Modeling Income in the Near Term (MINT) model.
PV = present value; CPI = consumer price index.
Median shared-benefit replacement rates, by shared lifetime earnings quintile for retired beneficiaries aged sixty-four to sixty-six in 2005 under alternative definitions of preretirement earnings (in percent).

A worker's Social Security benefit is determined by a Primary Insurance Amount (PIA) formula that favors low-wage earners. The formula is weighted so that lower-income workers get a higher replacement rate of their preretirement income than higher-income workers. This is not a higher benefit but a higher replacement rate. According to the Social Security Administration, large numbers of retirees depend on Social Security as a major source of their retirement income. Some statistics they quoted are:

- For one in five retirees, Social Security is their only source of retirement income.

- For one in three retirees, Social Security is 90 percent of their retirement income.

- For two in three retirees, Social Security is more than 50 percent of their retirement income.

A second problem with Social Security is that the monthly payments only go up if there is inflation. Cost-of-living increases with Social Security are not a given—even when the cost of living obviously has gone up. As I write this, Social Security has not had a cost-of-living increase in two years, but we all know that the prices are higher at the grocery store, the packaging sizes keep getting smaller, and our insurance premiums are rising every year. The problem is that increases in Social Security benefits are tied to how the government defines inflation, and the government's definition does not include food and fuel—two things that may well increase in cost and that everybody has to have.

In today's absence of pensions or adequate Social Security—two of the three legs of the stool—we need to plan for our own retirement. We must figure out how much we'll need every month and where that money will be coming from. We want to stay independent and keep our income similar to what it was when we were working.

Ideally, five to ten years before we retire, we've accumulated a nest egg from savings or inheritance or have liquidated a business. Now we have to take that money and make it last who knows how long—hopefully many, many years.

This wasn't always the case. Back in 1982, when I worked at General Motors in the personnel department, I saw that the average number of monthly checks a Pontiac retiree received was thirteen. That meant people lived only an average of thirteen months after retirement! We used to work until we were sixty-five and then tend to die at sixty-seven. Now we are working until sixty or sixty-five, and it is not unrealistic to count on living to eighty-five or longer.

While the increased lifespan may seem like a blessing, it is only wonderful if we are healthy, still living life on our own, and still have money to do the things that we enjoy doing. And we don't want to work until we're eighty-five. We want to take ten, fifteen, or twenty years and enjoy being able to travel, see our grandkids, or pursue whatever other goals we have for our retirement. When it comes down to it, I believe we all need a plan whose success is not determined by whether we retire in a good year—like the physician I spoke of earlier—or in a bad year. In designing Piece by Piece™, I made an effort to provide a framework help to generate income even when retirees are faced with economic volatility at the time they retire—and beyond.

WHEN SHOULD YOU START TO THINK ABOUT RETIREMENT INCOME?

The *accumulation phase* of retirement saving, between age twenty (or whenever you start those working years) and around fifty, are great years. If you're lucky, your employers match your contributions into a retirement plan like a 401(k). You may get an inheritance. In short, you tend to build up a nest egg.

Keep in mind that there is no assurance that any strategy will ultimately be successful or profitable nor protect against a loss.

This phase typically allows you to concentrate on growth as you accumulate and save what you can. It typically doesn't matter quite so much how the money is invested, because you have time on your side. The risk tends to be lower; you may be able to handle the movements in the market and still feel confident because you are not planning on retiring in the next decade. The goal is for things to smooth out over time.

When you retire, you enter the *utilization stage*. Your focus changes from growth to income-stream generation. This is the point where you typically have to start pulling money out of your nest egg for your income. If you're lucky enough to have a pension, that's great. Social Security income is also helpful. However, as we discussed, most of us will need more than our Social Security payments to live on. We need a plan to utilize our nest egg so that it may last as long as we do. Since we're basically creating our own retirement paycheck, the risk is typically much higher than it was in the accumulation phase; after all, a mistake could cost five years of income.

This utilization stage requires adjustments in your portfolio because you do not want to draw down too much money too quickly. When you change over your 401(k) or other accumulation vehicle to a utilization orientation, you have to look at completely different mechanisms for generating income. Instead of investing in things that are just growing, as you did in the accumulation phase, you need to find things that are producing a nice framework of income that you can potentially live on—and not outlive.

The timing of these phases is different for everyone. For example, by the time you turn fifty, you may realize that it's not as much fun working as it has been in the past. You may be thinking that you'd like to work fewer hours—or even start thinking about retirement.

On the other hand, you may love your career and be happy to work well into your sixties.

For many people, establishing a plan for retirement ten years before you'd actually like to retire is ideal! The goal is to give your money more time to grow. If you wait until the last minute to set things up—say, at age sixty-two or sixty-five—you may have missed the opportunity to allow your money to work for you by putting a framework together to generate a plan of reinvested dividends and interest. However, even if you only have five to seven years before you would like to retire, there may still be time to work with your nest egg to create your later income stream. Even if things did not go as well as you'd hoped—maybe you did not have the returns you'd expected, because the market was disappointing—you are still working. You may have to extend your working life by a couple of years, but it's doable.

Obviously, if you come to see me when you're sixty-four and one-half and you want to retire at sixty-five, there are few options we can put into place to improve your income stream. We will find ways to help you to retire, but it's not as easy or successful as when you give us five to ten years to work together with you.

As you can see in this chart on the next page, the government wants you to start thinking about retirement around age fifty. The IRS gives you an incentive, at the time you turn fifty, by allowing you to put extra catch-up money into your retirement plan. It's different for every program, but as an example, instead of allowing you to put $5,500 into your IRA, the IRS lets you put in an extra $1,000 or $6,500. This is a great opportunity, although it can be tough if you're paying off a house, raising a family, or making college payments.

Keep in mind that there is no assurance that any strategy will ultimately be successful or profitable nor protect against a loss.

Eligible for IRA and 401(k) catch-up provisions **50**

55 Eligible for penalty free separation-from-service withdrawals from 401(k)s

Eligible to begin withdrawing from IRAs and 401(k)s penalty free **59**1/2

62 First eligible for Social Security with reduced benefits

First eligible for Medicare **65**

66 Full retirement age (FRA) for Social Security (born 1943-1954; FRA increases by two month for every year from 1955 to 1959)

Full retirement age for Social Security (born 1960 or later) **67**

70 Maximum Social Security benefit (you must begin taking benefits)

Required minimum distributions begin the year after you hit this age **70**1/2

If you decide you'd like to retire at age fifty-five, you can take a separation from service, leaving your employer in some fashion and start utilizing your 403(b) or 457 retirement resources without any penalty. This applies to people who work for a school system or the government. There are also mechanisms in the tax code, specifically 72t, that exempt workers from penalties. Hardship distributions also have exceptions that reduce or eliminate penalties. This is where a person needs tax and financial advice before making any decisions that might trigger a negative event with IRS consequences.

Age fifty-nine and a half is the magic day when you can start pulling money out of your IRAs and 401(k)s without penalties—which earlier could be as high as 5 or 10 percent.

Sixty-two is another magical milestone—the first opportunity that the government gives us to access our Social Security benefits. But if you do retire early at sixty-two and start pulling out your benefits, you'll take a pretty good cut in benefits. Since the government figures that they are going to be paying you over more years, you will get about 75 percent of what your benefit would have been if you had waited until your full retirement age.

Your full retirement age—the age at which you'll get 100 percent of your Social Security benefits—depends on when you were born. If you were born prior to 1943, it is age sixty-five. It's age sixty-six or sixty-seven for most of us now. And if you don't collect Social Security until age seventy, which is the maximum amount of time you can wait, the government gives you an 8 percent rate of return. In any case, you must begin taking benefits at age seventy.

Sixty-five is the magic age for Medicare. *This is very important.* If you retire before you're sixty-five and do not receive health care during retirement from your former employer, you will have to purchase your own health insurance. You can expect to pay premiums of between $1,000 and $1,500 a month, depending on where you are in the country and how much your deductible is; this can eat up most of your Social Security benefits. In addition, out-of-pocket health-care expenses can add up fast. I still advise my clients to plan on $150 a month for supplemental coverage and then to remember that even with supplemental health care, there are going to be some out-of-pocket expenses.

At seventy and one-half, as the physician found out, the IRS requires you to start taking an RMD from your 401(k) or IRA. The amount can be pretty hefty, too. Add to that the fact that your account may be going down in bad economic times (such as 2000–2002 or 2007–2008), and you may find you've lost significant funds in a couple of years. It can really hurt your nest egg. The government's reasoning is that it has given you the opportunity to save, but now you're getting older and have not paid any taxes on that money. They want to make sure that you pay taxes on it before you leave this life.

All of these factors emphasize the importance of beginning your retirement plan at least ten years before you decide to retire. We can help set up a solid foundation for retirement income that does not depend on what the market is doing or the state of the economy.

One of the potentially beneficial parts of this retirement foundation plan is *compounding*—a mathematical concept that helps savers potentially earn more. Compounding is basically "interest to earn interest"—you receive interest on the actual money you've invested (your principle) and, as a bonus, interest on your interest from past periods. This allows your nest egg to potentially grow much more quickly. If interest is compounding at 7.2 percent, your money doubles every ten years.* This is called the *Rule of 72*. Even more

---

*This is a hypothetical illustration and is not intended to reflect the actual performance of any particular security. Future performance cannot be guaranteed and individual investor's results will vary. Investing involves risk and you may incur a profit or loss regardless of the strategy selected.

amazing is the fact that compounding can occur whether the market goes up or down or bonds go up or down. So when you're fifty-five, we could pull some money out of your nest egg, set it aside, and start the clock ticking on that ten-year potential doubling of your money in time for your sixty-fifth birthday. It is a powerful tool to put to work for you.

With the concept of compounding in mind, let's say you are able to take an in-service withdrawal from a company plan at age fifty-five and plan on working for ten more years. We can put that income into investments that could potentially double in that amount of time. If you invest $100,000 in an investment that guarantees you the ability to pull a 5 percent withdrawal out—a *guaranteed-income product*— you would get $5,000 a year. But if you put in that $100,000 when you're fifty-five and it doubles to $200,000 by the time you're sixty-five, then that same 5 percent will be $10,000 a year for you when you retire*.

Just make sure to give yourself the gift of retirement planning *well before you retire* to help reap the most benefits.

A SPECIAL NOTE FOR SMALL BUSINESS OWNERS

Business owners want to help their employees retire. They sponsor retirement plans, put matching funds in 401(k) accounts, and so on. They offer seminars to employees to help them build up their nest eggs and plan for their retirement. In short, business owners see helping employees retire as a benefit that is important in employee recruitment and retention.

---

*This is a hypothetical illustration and is not intended to reflect the actual performance of any particular security. Future performance cannot be guaranteed and individual investor's results will vary. Investing involves risk and you may incur a profit or loss regardless of the strategy selected.

At the same time, independent business owners often tell me that they don't need to save for their own retirement. They say they will just sell their business when the time comes, or they will always enjoy doing side jobs to supplement their Social Security: "I can't imagine not always doing this." That's nice if it works out and if you're able to maintain good health. Just one day after we had a similar discussion, a client, who is an electrician, was working on a big job at a junior high school. He got up onto a turned-over five-gallon bucket to reach for something, then he forgot where he was, stepped off, fell, and hurt his back. Accidents can happen. And even if they do not happen to you, they can happen to a spouse or one of your children. If an accident is serious enough, you may even need to retire or cut down on working hours in order to care for the family member.

Accidents are not the only unforeseen challenges. For many small business owners, deciding to retire means transitioning out of the company—or selling it. Often, the business cannot be readily sold, at least not the exact day they want to retire! I have a client right now who is trying to sell his business, an auto repair facility; he has to retire because he has become disabled. One person was interested in buying the building, but the owner does not want to sell the building. He wants to sell the building along with the business to make sure his employees still have their jobs. This is an extremely challenging plan. Unless you have about ten years to look around for the right person to buy your business, you can't count on selling it. And the possibility exists that you may not be able to sell it at all. The business is dependent on the reputation and skills of the owner, and these may not be easily transferrable.

As a business owner, you are no doubt used to taking care of yourself. You are independent. You started with nothing. You have earned money, started your business, and succeeded. You may be thinking that if you have to start from scratch again, it will be no big deal. This may not be true twenty years down the road. You'll want a fallback plan for retirement. If you are able to do side jobs or you are able to sell the business, it's a bonus. But just in case, you need a plan.

As if those are not enough reasons, a retirement plan for yourself, such as an IRA or a 401(k), is a nice tax benefit for business owners. You can set a nest egg aside for yourself, and the business does not pay taxes on it. You will not pay taxes on it until you take it out after you are fifty-nine and a half. And you may be more confident when deciding whether you can sell your business or pick up part-time work long after you were ready to retire.

QUESTION AND ANSWER

I'm a small business owner; what business retirement plan should I consider?

There are many different types of plans to be considered, including: Simple IRAs, simplified employee pension (SEP) IRAs, 401(k)s (with or without a profit-sharing component including safe harbor, age-based, and new-comparability) and defined-benefit plans. The answer will depend on the overall goals of the plan (attracting employees, encouraging longevity, offering tax breaks, deferring owner income, etc.) as well as the characteristics of the business (including family employees, unionized employees, business structure, etc.). There are questionnaires available, which will allow an owner or human resources manager to assess the "fit" between a plan and the company.

CHAPTER 2

IT'S THE EGGS,
NOT THE HEN!

Retirement opens the door on a whole new portion of your life with nearly endless possibilities. Unfortunately, from a practical standpoint, you also lose your steady paycheck from your employer. Thus, our aim in retirement planning is to find a way to replace those steady monthly payments during your retirement, no matter what is happening in the market the year you retire and no matter how long you live.

STRATEGIES FOR CREATING A RETIREMENT PAYCHECK: YOUR HEN AND YOUR EGGS

The Piece by Piece™ retirement plan is specifically designed to address the concerns that cause clients the most anxiety. Such as: "When I retire, how am I going to create a retirement paycheck with my nest egg to replace my work paycheck?"

To answer this question, let's go back to the metaphor of a hen laying eggs: The idea is not to sell or kill the "hen" (the investments) to create your retirement income but to live off of the "eggs" (the interest and dividends).

The idea that governs the Piece by Piece™ plan is easy to understand:

- Your portfolio (the hen) is designed to generate some money (eggs).

- Your monthly statement reveals what your portfolio is worth at market that day, but when you retire, you likely care more about the income generated, which is what you can live on.

- Therefore, we want to concentrate not on what the hen is worth on a particular day but on how many eggs you can get to live on.

- You don't kill off the hen that provides the eggs.

In simple terms, Piece by Piece™ is designed to generate real income streams. The model strives to balance your income sources properly so that you will have a paycheck not only for the next few years but potentially throughout your retirement—for the rest of your life. To do this, your portfolio needs to generate your income. The portfolio could be constructed of stocks, bonds, rental houses, or anything that generates income. The statement that you get in the mail every month tells you how much your portfolio is worth that day, but that fact is only important if you are going to sell it that day. What's really important is that your portfolio keeps generating the money you need.

It's important to keep that monthly update from getting the best of you. When it comes to long-term financial planning, short-term reports can cause an information overload. At the end of the day or the month, you must receive a report on what that portfolio is worth, and that can be scary. Keep in mind, though, that you also have other assets that you need to utilize, like a car or a house, but you don't learn the price of those assets every day, so you can choose to ignore them. Those short-term reports are only important to help ensure that your portfolio stays relatively healthy and keeps producing that income. As long as you're getting the income that you need from other pieces of the portfolio, it does not matter as much if the value of the portfolio goes up a little, down a little, up a little, and down a little. As long as it is healthy, your hen potentially generates the eggs that you need when you need them.

TRADITIONAL MODELS OF RETIREMENT-INCOME PLANNING

As discussed in the introduction, there are three traditional models of retirement-income planning. They all worked pretty well in the

Keep in mind that there is no assurance that any strategy will ultimately be successful or profitable nor protect against a loss past, when people did not expect to live to more than sixty-seven or seventy. Today, though, with people living longer and longer, I believe each of the models has some flaws.

One retirement-income planning model is called the *bucket approach*. It segments your retirement life into a series of buckets, according to the decades of your life, and invests them accordingly. The first ten years (sixty to seventy years old), you have investments that are very liquid because you know you are going to be needing the money. In the middle stage (seventy to eighty years), you might have 50 percent stocks and 50 percent bonds. In the third and last stage (eighty to ninety years), you would have all growth or all stocks. The plan is for thirty years. The rationale behind the plan is that you are not going to be as upset about volatility twenty or thirty years out, because you know you will have the money to live on during the next few years.

The second retirement-income model is called the *systematic-withdrawal approach*. The financial advisor might say, "Take an asset allocation of (for simplicity's sake) 50 percent stocks and 50 percent bonds. If you need to take 3 percent off your portfolio every year to live on, we'll just take 3 percent of the stocks and 3 percent of the bonds and call it good." You arbitrarily and across the board take the same amount; you are not picking and choosing different investments. It's a systematic withdrawal of a certain percentage of your assets.

The third model might be called your *necessities-versus-luxuries*. You pay for all your necessities, like food and shelter, through a guaranteed income stream from things like Social Security and a pension. Then you pay for the luxuries—things like traveling or going out to dinner—from your savings or investments in a nonguaranteed account. As the value of this account changes, a client's ability to spend on the "luxuries" that year also changes.

Different planners have different names for these three models, but these three are the most common. Many financial planners study and adopt one of these, but the more I reviewed and utilized them, the more I was interested in designing a different type of framework that focused on how retirees spend their retirement dollars.

THE PROBLEMS WITH THE TRADITIONAL APPROACHES

The bucket approach is potentially challenging because it's so easy to say, "Let's ignore that third bucket that just lost 50 percent of its value because we know it will come back over those thirty years." But what if it *doesn't* get back to the expected level? We don't want to be a burden to our children, and we don't want to have to eat cat food. No matter how many times I say, "Don't worry," you'll see the statement, and you may worry. It's just human nature. Since monthly statements are generally not designed by designated buckets, clients have a tendency to simply view the overall return of their portfolio.

I believe the main flaw with the systematic-withdrawal approach is the decision which must be made on "how" to take the agreed-upon percentage, as an example, a 4 percent withdrawal. Using a $200,000 portfolio, there can be many variations:

- A straight 4 percent = $8,000

- Should the second year increase with inflation? Say 4.03 percent or $8,240?

- If the portfolio is $175,000 in year two, should the withdrawal be adjusted to $7,000 (4 percent times $175,000)?

Of course, over time, these decisions are amplified year after year until the longer-term results are very different. Depending on how these questions are answered, they will definitely affect the client's lifestyle and confidence. A retirement "paycheck" that gets smaller is difficult for anyone to swallow and not a scenario I want to be walking clients through quarter after quarter.

As for the third model, which separates necessities and luxuries, how do you define *necessity*? Do I really *need* to travel to see my grandkids? Do I ever *need* to go out to dinner? This plan doesn't plan for people to really *live* in their retirement. If you've lived an active life and have big goals for retirement, you likely won't want to be sixty-five and have no money to do anything but pay your bills and watch *The Price Is Right*.

As if those shortcomings were not bad enough, the traditional models have another major flaw in common: the market conditions of the year you retire can make a huge difference in how much money you will have for the rest of your life. This is called the *sequence of returns risk*. For example, 1995 was a good year to retire. If you retired in 2000, it was not so good.

The bucket approach might work if you retire in a bad year because you have cash in that first bucket for three to five years. But—and this is a huge but—it would depend on how much you earned in those other two later buckets. You will be pulling the money forward when it is only worth half as much. This could be detrimental for the long-term health of the portfolio.

With the systematic-withdrawal approach, you (and my physician client) may have pulled money out as the market was going down in 2001 and 2002, and you may have not yet recovered.

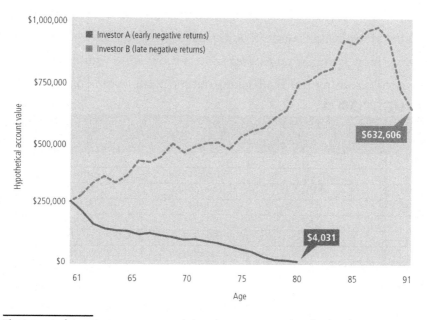

The impact of negative return years early in retirement can result in funds exhausting at a much earlier age than expected. (Source: MFS Investment Management) *This is a hypothetical illustration and is not intended to reflect the actual performance of any particular security. Future performance cannot be guaranteed and individual investor's results will vary.

The chart on the following page shows the sequence of returns for Investor A, who retired at age sixty-two in a bad year, with three years of negative returns in a row. Investor B also retired at age sixty-two but in a good year. It is important to note that Investors A and B had the same annual returns over thirty years, with each portfolio earning an average annual return of 6.6 percent, except that Investor A's annual returns were inverted to represent Investor B's annual returns.

Both plans began with $250,000 and had returns of 6.6 percent. Look at Investor A's hypothetical returns of -11, -18.5, -2.0, +4.5, +8.8, etc. It comes to 6.6 percent. And Investor B gets exactly the same returns, 6.6 percent. This time, though, the numbers are turned upside down, with the negative numbers at the end, That -11 return now comes to the investor at age ninety-one. While the overall, long-term return of both portfolios is 6.6 percent, and the 3 percent withdrawal rate is the same, the timing of the market's ups and downs makes for a very different outcome: having money to pass on as a legacy versus outliving your money. Both Investor A and Investor B are taking out 3 percent a year. For Investor A,

INVESTOR A

Age	Hypothetical **negative** early returns	Hypothetical account value	Annual withdrawal adjusted 3% for inflation
61		$250,000.00	
62	-11.2%	$209,500.00	$12,500.00
63	18.5%	$157,867.50	$12,875.00
64	-2.9	$140,028.09	$13,261.25
65	4.5%	$132,276.39	$13,659.03
66	8.8%	$130,276.39	$14,068.86
67	1.2%	$117,348.78	$14,490.93
68	17.4%	$122,841.82	$14,925.65
69	5.2%	$113,856.17	$15,373.42
70	7.6%	$106,674.61	$15,834.63
71	5.5%	$96,232.05	$16,309.66
72	19.9%	$98,583.27	$16,798.95
73	8.6%	$89,758.51	$17,302.92
74	11.2%	$81,989.46	$17,822.01
75	6.3%	$68,798.12	$18,356.67
76	8.5%	$55,738.59	$18,907.37
77	15.0%	$44,624.78	$19,474.59
78	-2.0%	$23,673.46	$20,058.83
79	4.3%	$4,030.82	$20,660.60
80	6.5%		
81	9.2%		
82	-4.2%		
83	16.3%		
84	9.0%		
85	2.3%		
86	21.1%		
87	13.4%		
88	-3.5%		
89	12.6%		
90	22.1%		
91	15.8%		

Keep in mind that there is no assurance that any strategy will ultimately be successful or profitable nor protect against a loss.

3 percent of $250,000 is $12,500, which means he is going to run out of money in eighteen years. But Investor B, who also started with $250,000, still had $632,606 left when he died at age ninety-one—more than thirty years later. (This is graphically displayed on page 35.)

INVESTOR B

Age	Hypothetical **positive** early returns	Hypothetical account value	Annual withdrawal adjusted 3% for inflation
61		$250,000.00	
62	15.8%	$277,000.00	$12,500.00
63	22.1%	$325,342.00	$12,875.00
64	12.6%	$353,073.84	$13,261.25
65	-3.5%	$327,057.17	$13,659.09
66	13.4%	$356,813.97	$14,068.86
67	21.1%	$417,610.79	$14,490.93
68	2.3%	$412,290.19	$14,925.65
69	9.0%	$434,022.88	$15,373.42
70	16.3%	$488,933.98	$15,834.63
71	-4.2%	$452,089.09	$16,309.66
72	9.2%	$476,822.33	$16,798.95
73	6.5%	$490,576.76	$17,302.92
74	4.3%	$493,849.55	$17,822.01
75	-2.0%	$465,615.89	$18,356.67
76	15.0%	$516,550.90	$18,907.37
77	8.5%	$540,983.13	$19,474.59
78	6.3%	$555,006.24	$20,058.83
79	11.2%	$596,506.35	$20,660.60
80	8.6%	$626,525.48	$21,280.41
81	19.9%	$729,285.22	$21,918.83
82	5.5%	$746,819.52	$22,576.39
83	7.6%	$780,324.12	$23,253.68
84	5.2%	$796,949.68	$23,951.29
85	17.4%	$910,949.10	$24,669.83
86	1.2%	$896,470.56	$25,409.93
87	8.8%	$949,187.74	$26,172.22
88	4.5%	$964,943.80	$26,957.39
89	**-2.9%**	$909,194.32	$27,766.11
90	**-18.5%**	$712,394.27	$28,599.10
91	**-11.2%**	$632,606.11	

Comparing gains versus losses in the early years of retirement on a hypothetical portfolio.

In other words, no matter what the market was like the year you might retire, you might make 6.6 percent as an average over the next thirty years. If you retired in a really bad year—say, 2000, 2001, or 2002—and had a negative return in the market for those first years, you would run out of money a lot sooner than if you had retired in what happened to be a rock 'n rollin' time for the market, as in the dot-com years.

Though this is a hypothetical example for illustrative purposes and is not intended to represent the future performance of any MFS product or actual market performance, this is essentially why I believe the systematic-withdrawal approach does not work. If you retire in a bad market year and take systematic withdrawals of just 3 percent, which is a really small amount, you might still run out of money—just because you retired in a bad year.

The necessities-versus-luxuries method *might* work better in a down market. The guaranteed income streams from pensions, Social Security, and so on would provide for the necessities. However, all luxuries may, by definition, be forgone until the market recovered and the nest egg had provided additional monies for the luxuries.

With Piece by Piece™, you get a hybrid approach that is designed to allow you to retire in any year, in any kind of market. It acknowledges that you are human and that you expect to enjoy your retirement. And it takes into account the fact that unforeseen things are going to happen in your life. Because—let's face it—retirement is more than just a math problem, it's a lifestyle. And in planning your retirement, Piece by Piece™ is designed to allow you the flexibility to enjoy your retirement years, be more confident through volatile markets, and cover emergencies and at least some luxuries.

In my opinion, more than other retirement utilization plans, Piece by Piece™ is specifically tailored to your lifestyle. Together, we develop a personalized plan to segment your nest egg—a combination of your investments, rollovers, pensions, Social Security, and annuities—into three pieces, each with a distinct goal:

1. Income Today: A piece designed to create the income you will require during each of your retirement years, no matter how long you live. We generally put 40–60 percent of your nest egg in this portion and aim to give you a monthly check based on your paycheck before retirement.

2. Income Tomorrow: A piece designed to create increased income for inflation, health care, or special needs along the way. Income Tomorrow is especially helpful for people without a pension, which is becoming increasingly common. We may recommend creating your own self-pension through an insurance company, called an *annuity*—an income guaranteed to not go away. You have insurance on your house and insurance on your car. Your nest egg is often worth more than your house or car, so it is worth insuring as well. I generally recommend putting 20–30 percent of your nest egg in Income Tomorrow.

3. Flexibility Dollars: A piece for flexibility—provisions to pay for those unknown, unforeseen things that may face you around any corner—because some things just cannot be planned for. Maybe you have grandkids who are born in Thailand, and you want to go there and meet them. You don't want to look at that as a luxury. You want to treat it as something that happened that you did not expect to happen back when you were planning for retirement—but you still want to have the money to cover it. We'll normally have 10–25 percent of your nest egg in Flexibility Dollars.

INCOME TOMORROW	FLEXIBILITY DOLLARS
INCOME TODAY	

With this plan, if you have a negative return early in retirement because you picked a bad year to retire, it may not affect your lifestyle for the next thirty years. Or, when the market is down and the television is full of doom and gloom, you realize that you have a plan. Every month, your portfolio is designed to continue to generate income (through interest, dividends, rents, income, etc.) as initially planned. The value of your portfolio may be worth more or less, but—and this is very important—you should still have an income stream. If you should need more income for some reason, you can begin using the Income Tomorrow piece and may even have some flexibility if you need it. Such a backup plan is not factored into the traditional financial-planning approaches.

The Piece by Piece™ plan adjusts to accommodate for your own personality and spending behavior. People usually do not change just because they retire. If we plan for you to receive a regular income check that is the same as before retirement, you are probably going to do the same thing with the money that you did with it when you were working. You can save some of it, or you can spend it as you wish. All I'm doing is sending you the cash. If you clip coupons, you're probably going to keep on clipping coupons. If you like to eat out, you're probably still going to enjoy that. Retirement is supposed

---

Keep in mind that there is no assurance that any strategy will ultimately be successful or profitable nor protect against a loss. Dividends are not guaranteed and must be authorized by the company's board of directors.

to be the time we are able to do some of the things that we put off doing when we were raising our families, working, and paying off the house. We want to be able to enjoy it and not feel guilty that we're spending our nest egg on "luxuries."

By creating the plan together, we can help you not only potentially generate the money you will need, it also ensures that all of the plan's details make sense to you. I have heard that some financial advisors may talk in generalities, pat you on the head, and send you on your way. I can't work that way—we will take all the time you need in order to understand how I am working with your money.

In the upcoming chapters, I will talk about each of the three pieces and how we work together to personalize each one. For now, what is important to know is that the Piece by Piece™ plan is designed to allow you to be more confident in low interest rate environments and through market volatility. No matter the market, my goal is to send you your check every month, just like when you were working, to give you something to live on (Income Today). Your plan will be designed to generate real income streams through the use of commonsense investments. In addition, it will have a backup plan (Income Tomorrow), as well as cash (Flexibility Dollars) for unforeseen financial needs. After all, we all need a new furnace—or just a treat—now and then.

QUESTION AND ANSWER

When should I get worried about a shrinking portfolio value (my hen)?

Of course, the answer to this is specific to each individual. I recommend the client and advisor determine this at the start of the financial-planning engagement. Normal market volatility of 10 percent can be expected as a usual event. Many clients put stop orders of 20 percent as the bottom of their comfort zone. I have one client who is sensitive to market volatility and has a limit at 7 percent on the downside.

Where can I find more information on the bucket approach?

This approach is explained in a October 2013 article by Christine Benz (of Morningstar fame), compliments of the American Association of Individual Investors (AAII). Many investments clubs use the AAII resources available on the website as well.

Where can I find more information regarding the systematic-withdrawal approach?

Each mutual fund company and annuity provider will generally have more information regarding taking regular withdrawals from their investment offerings. The American Funds website has a hypothetical example of removing 5 percent from a Capital Income Builder fund with an additional 3 percent each year for inflation protection, and I find it quite helpful. Remember that past performance does not guarantee future results. Also, make sure that you read and understand the company's website, and watch out for any perceived guarantees.

Where can I find more information on the necessities-versus-luxuries approach?

The following diagram is courtesy of Raymond James. It's a good way to look at the "needs or wants" categories and align them with retirement-income sources (such as pensions, social security, qualified income, etc.).

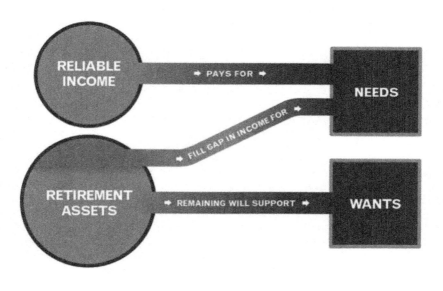

CHAPTER 3

INCOME TODAY: STRATEGIES FOR YOUR PAYCHECK IN RETIREMENT

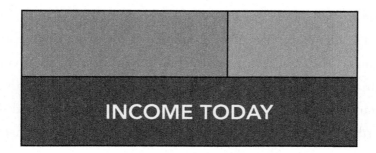

INCOME TODAY

T he Income Today component of the Piece by Piece™ retirement plan is designed to provide your monthly "paycheck" from stock dividends and interest generated from bonds,

Dividends are not guaranteed and must be authorized by the company's board of directors.

in addition to other income sources that might have been included in the plan (rental income, covered-call income, etc.). These income sources are balanced so that you should continue to get a paycheck not only over the first few years but throughout your retirement. All plans are a little different, but approximately 40–60 percent of your nest egg will be in the Income Today component.

Our exploration of Income Today begins with stories about some of my clients to illustrate how the amount in this piece of the retirement plan might differ depending on personal circumstances, spending habits, retirement age, and how many years before retirement we begin to work on their plans.

A SURPRISE RETIREMENT

John was fifty-five when his employer, a large utility company, offered him early retirement as a way to get some of the higher-paid supervisors to leave. If he accepted, the company would pay his health-care premiums until he was sixty-five and eligible for Medicare. They would not pay his wife's health care, though. John asked me, "What do you think I should do? I'm not really ready to retire."

"I'm afraid that since this is an at-will work state, once they tap you on the shoulder, you might as well go," I said. "They could terminate your employment tomorrow and not give you anything. Keep in mind that they are willing to give you health care, and that is worth a thousand dollars a month. If they are willing to do that for ten years, it's a nice bonus."

John had no pension, but his company had put a 4 percent match into his 401(k) while he was working there. Even so, he was worried about having enough money to live on if he retired ten years earlier than he had planned.

We sat down together and developed a Piece by Piece™ plan for him. First, we rolled over his 401(k) into a self-directed IRA. Since he would not be eligible for Social Security benefits until he was sixty-two, we put about 10 percent more money than the usual 40–60 percent in Income Today because we knew that he would have to draw on that portion for more of his "paycheck" until he hit sixty-two.

When he turned sixty-two, we dropped the amount in Income Today by the amount of Social Security that he got and redistributed the funds into Flexibility Dollars. We reduced his monthly Income Today paycheck back to 3 percent of the draw so that we could build up the Income Today portion. Instead of paying the interest and dividends out as John's monthly check, he began reinvesting the income and dividends and purchasing more shares. This will allow John to potentially recover some of his Income Today investments and have the opportunity to increase his monthly paycheck again in the future. In this way, he still has Income Today. John also had a backup plan (Income Tomorrow, discussed in chapter 4) and some flexibility, too (Flexibility Dollars, discussed in chapter 5).

JOHN'S PIECE BY PIECE™ PLAN

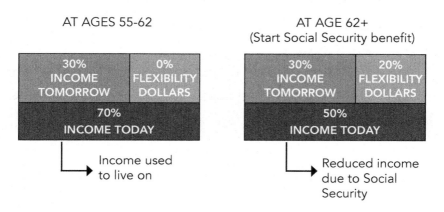

AT AGES 55-62

AT AGE 62+
(Start Social Security benefit)

30% INCOME TOMORROW	0% FLEXIBILITY DOLLARS
70% INCOME TODAY	

Income used to live on

30% INCOME TOMORROW	20% FLEXIBILITY DOLLARS
50% INCOME TODAY	

Reduced income due to Social Security

Keep in mind that there is no assurance that any strategy will ultimately be successful or profitable nor protect against a loss.

THE BENEFITS OF EARLY PLANNING

Juanita and Sebastian's story is a little different. I worked with the couple on their spousal IRAs; the total in the two was only $12,000 when they came to see me. When Juanita was forty-nine and Sebastian was fifty, he called and announced: "I can roll over my pension as a lump sum, and I want to do that. I really don't trust my employer to manage the money."

His announcement was a surprise because that is not normally how pensions work. Sometimes you can roll over the contributions you made to your 401(k) but not your pension (generally employer contributions). Sebastian insisted, though, that he could roll over his pension now, and then he could roll over his 401(k) when he left employment.

He came in, eager to work it out. His job took him on the high seas—thirty days on ship, then thirty days off. He wanted to have his plans in good order in case something happened to him when he was on ship. We put together a proposal for Income Today, Income Tomorrow, and some Flexibility Dollars. We still filled all three categories, but because he was still working, we reinvested all of the earnings from Income Today rather than drawing from it every month as a "paycheck."

Sebastian worked another ten years after he and his wife set up the plan, retiring at age sixty. During those years, he just added to the holdings that he already had.

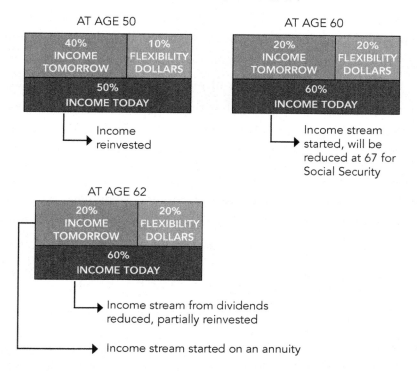

JUANITA AND SEBASTIAN'S PIECE BY PIECE™ PLAN

AT AGE 50

40% INCOME TOMORROW	10% FLEXIBILITY DOLLARS
50% INCOME TODAY	

→ Income reinvested

AT AGE 60

20% INCOME TOMORROW	20% FLEXIBILITY DOLLARS
60% INCOME TODAY	

→ Income stream started, will be reduced at 67 for Social Security

AT AGE 62

20% INCOME TOMORROW	20% FLEXIBILITY DOLLARS
60% INCOME TODAY	

→ Income stream from dividends reduced, partially reinvested

→ Income stream started on an annuity

DECIDING TO CONTINUE THE WORKING LIFE

When Dominic came to develop his plan before retirement, he had just left an oil-services company that went bankrupt. He was able to get his pension, but it was very small, and he was not able to roll it over. Thus, that pension became the Income Today piece. But at $500 a month, it was not enough to live on, and he was too young to draw on his Social Security benefit.

Dividends are not guaranteed and must be authorized by the company's board of directors.

Dominic had been saving in his company's 401(k) plan. These investments could be rolled over into a self-directed IRA, where his Piece by Piece™ plan could be custom-designed by he and I. In order to provide Dominic with income, he supplemented his small pension with income-generating investments in his Income Today piece.

Luckily, Dominic was only fifty-six, and he was not at all ready to retire. He was able to get a job with a competitor, and his wife was also still working. Then, when he retired, we reshuffled the assets in the three pieces. At sixty-two, Dominic was able to draw on his Social Security benefit. This allowed him to greatly reduce the income from his Income Today piece to help provide for his current living expenses. The investments that had been used to generate income could now be redeployed to Income Tomorrow and Flexibility Dollars pieces.

DOMINIC'S PIECE BY PIECE™ PLAN

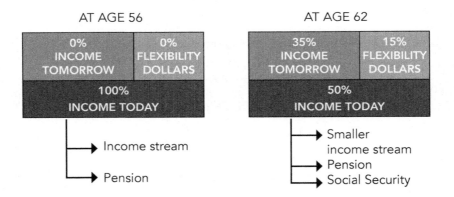

WHEN SPOUSES RETIRE AT DIFFERENT TIMES

Anne, a preschool teacher, was finding it more and more difficult to get up off the floor where she worked with the children. So at sixty-two, as soon as she was eligible for Social Security, she decided to retire. She also had a pension from the school system and a 403(b). Her husband, George, though, was not ready to stop working.

With Anne retired, they were able to live off George's current paycheck and Anne's pension check and did not need to augment their Income Today piece. They elected to wait to use their Income Today piece until they both were retired. Meanwhile, we rolled her 403(b) into Income Tomorrow and Flexibility Dollars.

George turned sixty-four and will be retiring at the end of the year. We will be adding his Social Security benefits to Income Today, and he will roll over his 401(k) into their Income Today piece, where we can invest it to earn dividends and interest, as well as fund his Income Tomorrow and Flexibility Dollar pieces.

ANNE AND GEORGE'S PIECE BY PIECE™ PLAN

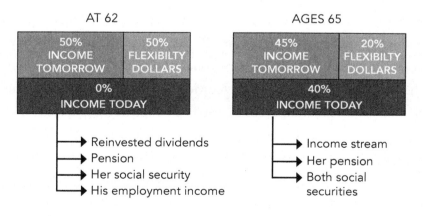

Dividends are not guaranteed and must be authorized by the company's board of directors. Keep in mind that there is no assurance that any strategy will ultimately be successful or profitable nor protect against a loss.

THE HEALTH-CARE COMPONENT
OF INCOME TODAY

We all know that health care is expensive, and it's importance in our lives often increases as we get older.

If you retire at age sixty-five, before you are eligible for Medicare coverage, health-care insurance premiums will take a large portion out of your retirement Income Today check. A couple would typically pay $1,200 to $1,500 a month for their combined health care before Medicare, and that is for a plan with extremely high deductibles and out-of-pocket expenses. People who have had employer-based health insurance until retirement often do not realize how high the costs for health care can be once they are no longer covered by the company's plan. Health-care premiums for an individual under sixty-five can easily eat up the entire Social Security check, and one must also reserve a large amount of money for out-of-pocket medical expenses due to the huge deductibles.

Any individual or couple planning on retiring before receiving Medicare benefits must have a plan for this large expense. I recommend a separate savings account (or health-care savings account if you have access to one) with a lump sum equal to $1,500 per month times the number of months prior to Medicare benefit eligibility plus $10,000 for deductibles. For example, a couple retiring at sixty-two and eligible for Medicare at sixty-five would need $64,000 set aside for health-care expenses ($1,500 x 36 + $10,000).

To offset this burden, you may be eligible to receive Affordable Care Act subsidies; the rules are the same whether or not you are retired. I worked with a couple, Rita and Fred, who both retired at age sixty-four last year at the end of the summer. They couldn't wait to get right in their RV and start traveling. They were able to postpone withdrawing from their Income Today piece because they had $80,000 in a savings account. They would be able to live on this for twelve to twenty-four months, depending on their health-care premiums. They claimed Fred's Social Security benefits, which provided about $18,000 of annual income. They applied for health care through the Marketplace and received a subsidy due to their low income. They used their savings to supplement their living expenses and are happily RVing around the United States during their first two years of retirement.

Rita called me in December because they were both going to turn sixty-five later the next year and wanted to look into any changes in their retirement plan that should be tended to. They also asked me to continue holding off giving them their Income Today retirement checks; the health-care subsidy was advantageous, and they would lose it if their income went up.

Now that they have drawn down their savings account, this summer Rita and Fred will begin utilizing the income from their Income Today piece. Both of them turned sixty-five last fall, qualified for Medicare and began Social Security benefits.

INVESTMENTS IN INCOME TODAY

The money in the Income Today piece of the plan is designed to supply you with a monthly paycheck that you can live on in retirement. To do that, we invest it in vehicles that have several characteristics. First, the investments in Income Today must pay a yield, anywhere from 3 percent to 10 percent. Second, the investments should be diversified. We do not want to put all our eggs in any one basket. And third, as another part of diversifying, the investments should be predicted to move in different directions.

Years ago, bonds were a great option. We had the good fortune to be able to say, "Here's a bond that pays 6 percent; we'll just use that for the rest of our lives." There were even times when interest rates were 8 percent, so we could just leave all the money in a money market. Interest rates have been low for a long time now, however, so retirement investing is more of a challenge today. We've had to get creative—the following are typical investments in retirement planning today:

- laddered CDs
- corporate bond funds
- low-quality bond funds
- international bond funds
- dividend-paying stock funds
- preferred stock funds
- convertible bond funds
- real estate investment trusts (REITs)
- cash-value life insurance loan
- infrastructure funds (pipelines, towers, ports, etc.)

- individual bonds
- municipal bond funds
- emerging-market bond funds
- individual dividend-paying stocks
- individual preferred stocks
- individual convertible bonds
- income-oriented exchange-traded funds (ETFs)
- fixed-income annuities
- equity-income funds
- master limited partnership (MLP) funds

There are a lot of options, and each has its own plusses and minuses. A client's tolerance for risk will be a big determining factor in what we

Diversification does not ensure a profit or guarantee against a loss. Dividends are not guaranteed and must be authorized by the company's board of directors.

put in the Income Today part of his or her individual portfolio. Just as every person I work with has different ways they want to use their money, every single person who has stepped into my office has an absolutely unique way of looking at the money that they have accumulated.

Regardless of their backgrounds and the amount of assets, I ask everyone the same question in our first meeting.

"How much does it bother you when you see your statement go up and down?"

I have heard a lot of different answers because everyone has a different propensity for risk. Some people want their money in a certificate of deposit (CD) or another vehicle that is insured and guaranteed. Even though it may be paying 1 percent, and even though that may be only $700 a month, they are determined to learn how to live on that. These investors do not want to worry about having to work during retirement or putting their money at risk. This approach is conservative but assists giving the client confidence in their plan.

Others may feel that the money they have accumulated is not enough to make a difference, and they would like to be very aggressive investing it. Every once in a while, I meet a client who wants to invest in a more aggressive portfolio, as was the case when I met Bernie and Jane. He had a pension, and they both had a Social Security benefit. Jane had a very small balance in an old retirement account. She wanted to aggressively invest the small amount in a biotechnology investment. Jane saw this money as having the potential to "hit a home run" and provide the ability to take a big vacation some day or splurge on a luxury. If the investment didn't work out so successively, she knew that they weren't depending on the money to live on for daily expenses.

Jane's approach is tougher to stomach when it's an entire nest egg. People who have saved and saved throughout their working lives can find it very difficult to see their balances going down as they begin to utilize those savings in retirement. I tell them that eventually they are going to have to use it; that is what it's here for. It's not terrible to use it; what would be terrible would be not having enough money to use.

Believe it or not, I find that people who made less money when they worked are often more comfortable in retirement than people who made more money. For people who have always been in the lower-income brackets, Social Security is going to step in and be a relatively larger percentage of their retirement income. Say they made $30,000 a year, so they are used to living on that and have chosen that number for their monthly paycheck in retirement ($2,500). If they get $1,800 a month as a Social Security benefit and I am able to potentially get them $1,000 additional a month in Income Today, their monthly $2,800 would be annual income of $33,600—even more than they earned during their working years. But a client who made $100,000 a year would get just $2,787.80 per month in Social Security, the top benefit at full retirement age. If I were able to potentially get them another $1,000 a month in Income Today, for almost $50,000 a year, the difference from $100,000 a year would still remain large. So, in general, people who have made less over time are actually acclimated better to retirement because Social Security provides a larger percentage of their income in retirement, and the gap between income before and after retirement is often much narrower.

STOCK DIVIDENDS

The Income Today portion of a portfolio usually includes stocks so that the dividends generated are part of the monthly paycheck. We do not count on their appreciation. If their share value goes up, that's great, but it's not necessary for the plan to work.

I often choose stock in non-US international companies because they have a history of paying larger dividends than US companies do. Examples might include an Italian electric company, a Mexican concrete company, or a Chinese phone company—all of which have a tendency to pay a larger percentage of their earnings in dividends to shareholders. The Income Today part of the plan shown in the following hypothetical graphic on page 61 has $40,000 invested in international company stock, with a yield of 4.2 percent in dividends.

This yield represents well over twice what we could get in the bond market, and there's also the chance that the value will go up. Of course, there is also a chance that it will go down. As long as we pick wisely and are able to diversify, though, there's potentially less chance for the entire portfolio to go down. International dividend-paying investments with this kind of risk might represent 20 percent of the money in the Income Today part of your portfolio.

REAL ESTATE AND INFRASTRUCTURE INVESTMENTS

Another component of Income Today investments would be some kind of real estate income. If you are the type of person who could make money by buying a rental-income house and easily face the challenges of maintenance, that's great. If not, we strive to purchase commercial or residential real estate investments with a 5 percent or 6 percent return. I believe things that generate an income stream in the form of rent are

Dividends are not guaranteed and must be authorized by the company's board of directors. Please note that international investing involves special risks, including currency fluctuations, differing financial accounting standards, and possible political and economic volatility. Diversification does not ensure a profit or guarantee against a loss. Keep in mind that there is not assurance that any strategy will ultimately be successful or profitable nor protect against a loss. Past performance is not a guarantee of future results.

suitable investments in this category: for example, student housing and plazas that rent to Home Depots and other big-box stores.

Another component of Income Today investment related to real estate is investment in infrastructure companies—companies that strive to generate income by collecting rent on pieces of infrastructure. Examples are bridges, tollways, ports, marinas, airports, pipelines, and storage tankers. An investor in a toll road or airport concourse typically receives rental income on these type of investments. Cell phone companies pay rent on the land where their towers are sitting. Billboard companies pay rent every month for that land.

These infrastructure investments generally don't depend on the health of the economy. In a bad economy, you get on the Ohio Turnpike with your Kia and might pay $7—and in a good economy, you drive your Cadillac on the Ohio Turnpike and might pay the same $7. In addition, money from these infrastructure investments is not specifically tied to interest rates. In the example in the hypothetical graphic on page 61, we have another $50,000 invested in infrastructure, and, at 4.0 percent, the yield is similar to that of international stocks.

The infrastructure component of Income Today also might include municipal bonds. Potentially suitable investments are bonds for structures that are tied to income streams. For example, municipalities have civic centers, pools, ice rinks, and senior centers that generate revenue through user fees and other income. When people use the pool, they pay $2; they pay $5 for a session of water aerobics. Bonds that are tied to actual pay-for-use tend to be less sensitive to the prevailing interest rate; people are going to swim whether interest rates are 2 percent or 5 percent.

Be advised that investments in real estate and in REITs have various risks, including possible lack of liquidity and devaluation based on adverse economic and regulatory changes. Additionally, investments in REITs will fluctuate with the value of the underlying properties and the price at redemption may be more or less than the original price paid. Dividends are not guaranteed.

STRATEGIC-INCOME COMPONENT

Investments in the strategic-income category—income generators that the portfolio manager believes represent a "good value" at a specific time—are a bit riskier, but we want them in the Income Today portfolio for diversification. We want things that tend to run opposite to the bond market—opposite to interest rates. One of the things that fits this description is lower quality bonds. They tend to move more in correlation with stocks than with bonds. Higher-risk bonds may include cable-company bonds, such as Comcast and Charter. With this risk typically comes higher income—4.21 percent in our hypothetical example on page 61, with another $50,000 invested in this category.

FLOATING-RATE (LIMITED-DURATION) FUNDS

Finally, the sample portfolio has $40,000 invested in floating-rate (limited-duration) investments with a yield of 3.31 percent. These are bonds or loans with a very short duration. The rates float, but they tend to float with current interest-rate changes. So if we keep them for a short time, as interest rates go up, the investment will potentially go up and be worth more.

We would not want to hold a 2 percent bond for thirty years, but we might be willing to hold a 2 percent bond for six months if it gives us more than a money market does. Or we might find an investment that is paying 5 percent but has only six months left because someone passed away. I like to have the Income Today part of the portfolio be at least 20 percent bonds.

INCOME TODAY: AN EXAMPLE

Throughout the rest of the book, we will be looking at the Piece by Piece™ method of retirement-income planning. Let's create a hypothetical individual who wants to use this approach—we'll use her as an example in later chapters. Meet Clara Client, and take a look at her background, goals, and finances.

	Current Situation	**Future Planning**
Status	Single	
Age	60	Wants to retire at age 65
Wages	$75,000/year	Wants $60,000/year pre-tax
401k-employee contribution	9% (or $6,750)	
401k-employer match	3% (or $2,250)	
Social Security estimate		$2,000/mo @ 65
Financial Accounts		
Savings	$15,000	
401k	$600,000	
Roth IRA	$40,000	

When Clara Client arrives at her initial retirement-planning session at age sixty (five years prior to wanting to retire), she has a $600,000 retirement plan (401k) at her employer. The summary-plan document allows her to roll over her balance at age sixty to a self-directed IRA. We discuss her income needs and decide to invest $400,000 in the investments above.

CLARA CLIENT

A Piece by Piece™ of Income Today might include:

	$ Invested	Yield	Estimated Annual Income
Global Stocks	$30,000	4.16%	$1,248
US Stocks	$30,000	2.46%	$738
Income Investments	$50,000	5.08%	$2,540
Intl. Dividend Stocks	$40,000	4.20%	$1,680
Floating Rates	$40,000	3.31%	$1,324
Strategic Income	$50,000	4.21%	$2,105
High Income Bonds	$60,000	8.80%	$5,280
REIT Income	$50,000	5.25%	$2,625
Infrastructure	$50,000	4.00%	$2,000
	$400,000	4.89%	$19,540

$19,540/year estimated income—or 4.89%

Current yield—$19,540/12 months = $1,628/month

Estimated future income—5 years at 5% compound interest = $510,000 or $25,500/year

This is a hypothetical illustration and is not intended to reflect the actual performance of any particular security. Future performance cannot be guaranteed and investment yields will fluctuate with market conditions. Individual investor's results will vary. Dividends are not guaranteed and must be authorized by the company's board of directors.

The investments are diversified and yielding almost 5 percent. This interest and the dividends will be reinvested to purchase more shares for the next five years, until Clara reaches age sixty-five, when she wants to retire. In five years, with reinvested dividends and interest, we can assume that Clara's account balance might be $510,000. This assumes a flat market and 5 percent compounded interest.

So without adding any additional money to her IRA, Clara can expect income of $25,500 (5 percent x $510,000). If Clara's Social Security benefit is $2,000 per month (or $24,000 per year), then her Income Today piece will be almost $50,000 annually. This is a replacement ratio of 83 percent (retirement income estimate of $50,000/$60,000 net current wage).

INCOME TODAY

To help you understand how Income Today might work, the hypothetical graphic on page 61 shows the Income Today part of the plan created for Clara. On December 1, I would start issuing a check each month for $1,628. On the first of each month, that amount would be direct deposited in Clara's bank account. At $1,628 times twelve months of the year, the estimated income would be $19,540 for the next year.

Note that the $1,628 per month is before income taxes are taken out. When you sign up for Social Security, you can choose to take taxes out, or you can choose not to and pay it at the end of the year. In any case, you'll be paying taxes on your Social Security and your Income Today income at your normal marginal tax rate. Some people use their monthly Income Today paycheck to cover the taxes on their other income. For example, one of my clients got $400 in Income Today every month. He asked me to send all of it to the IRS every month to cover the taxes he was not withholding from his railroad pension and Social Security.

The Clara Client hypothetical graphic on page 61 shows that Social Security would start on January 1—about $2,000 a month. This sum also would be direct deposited into the bank account. This person would get another $24,000 a year in Social Security payments.

I had a client with a plan very similar to Clara's example, but when this client saw his plan, he requested some changes. He wanted to take all the international dividends (at 4.2 percent) and all the infrastructure dividends (at 4.0 percent) for the first year, reinvest them, and buy more shares. The goal was to make sure that next year's Income Today paycheck would be higher because he would have more shares generating dividends. Meanwhile, he was expecting an inheritance of $50,000, which would give him a cushion.

Dividends are not guaranteed and must be authorized by the company's board of directors.

QUESTION AND ANSWER

Are there really investments that pay 5 percent?

Yes, there are! Unfortunately, traditional bonds may not provide 5 percent, but there are numerous investment managers who have acknowledged this income challenge and have developed portfolios which distribute a higher yield than what would be available in the current low-interest rate market. Managers are looking to rents (from student housing, airport terminals, cell towers, ports, toll roads, etc.), international bonds (which may be higher at some point in time), and other innovative ideas to generate income for retirees.

What about junk bonds?

"Junk" bonds are typically those bonds which have lower-quality ratings and therefore require higher yields to compensate investors for risk. Historically, corporate default rates have been around 4 percent. Portfolios that purchase numerous bonds and diversify (by location, type of issuer, time to maturity, etc.) might be a sounder plan than trying to purchase these individually. Bond managers tend to have years of experience in research, which an advisor or smaller investor would find difficult to match.

CHAPTER 4

INCOME TOMORROW: YOUR BACKUP PLAN

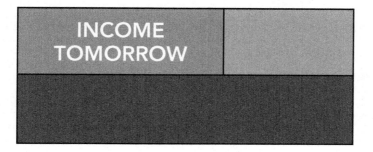

I ncome Tomorrow is designed to replace the Income Today piece of your retirement plan in the event that you experience an unhappy surprise: a decrease in income due to lower oil prices, reduced rents, eliminated corporate dividends, etc. Maybe you've been getting $5,000 in income every month, but now you are down to $3,000 a month. Of course, we hope this does not happen, but if it does, Income Tomorrow is your backup plan. We'll use it to help get your income stream back up to that $5,000 mark.

In the "good old days," when interest rates were 8 percent, we could just put your entire retirement savings in a bank CD. That 8 percent was guaranteed for five, ten, or twenty years down the road. Unfortunately interest rates aren't currently 8 percent. Many of my clients put 20–50 percent of the money from their portfolios into this piece, where the investments tend to be less volatile.

The amount in the Income Tomorrow piece varies greatly from person to person, however. If you have a good pension, your Income Tomorrow piece can be much smaller than that of someone with no guaranteed pension. If you have a pension, we might move most of this piece into your Flexibility Dollars piece. Or you might decide to put an extra 20 percent or 30 percent in Income Today and the rest in Flexibility Dollars.

For many people with pensions, though, having an Income Tomorrow piece may still be a good idea, since there's always a chance that the pension plan defaults. How much we decide to put in this piece depends on factors like how much money you have, whether or not you have been divorced, or whether or not you expect to have something coming from an inheritance.

USES FOR INCOME TOMORROW

This Income Tomorrow piece, then, is your backup plan in case a larger monthly amount is needed for your current lifestyle—or if dividends and income have been reduced. Maybe something happens in your life and you find that you need more income than we'd anticipated when we set up your plan. Or maybe you get a potentially debilitating disease like Parkinson's and decide that you would like to start enjoying an income while you can still get around easily. Or perhaps inflation has begun to erode the value of today's dollars and we need to supplement them.

Some clients decide to let the money in their Income Tomorrow piece have the potential to continue to grow. Others have chosen to turn on the income stream in that piece and spend the income streams from both Income Today and Income Tomorrow rather than reinvesting them. Still others find they are not spending as much as they predicted they would in their retirement years, or they have decided to pick up a part-time job, or perhaps they have received an inheritance. This increase in their current income leads them to decide to reinvest the income for Income Today and also put Income Tomorrow on hold until a future date.

These are not my decisions; they are completely up to each client. I have to admit that there have been times when I would have loved to tell people that they really should go ahead and replace the carpeting; they have the money. But it is their call, just like it was when they were working. Everybody has his or her own way of looking at money, and I respect that.

INVESTMENTS IN INCOME TOMORROW

Income Tomorrow investments usually consist of annuities. Other options are insured bonds and Treasury bonds. The mix depends on the needs and preferences of the individual client.

Most people have an opinion about annuities—good or bad. An annuity is simply an investment product sponsored by an insurance company (as opposed to a mutual fund company). The insurance company part is important. This gives a financial product a value that is guaranteed by the insurance company. Clients typically choose annuities because they want an investment product with *guarantees*. The guarantees are only as good as the insurance company's balance sheet, though, as all guarantees are backed by the claims-paying ability of the specific company.

An annuity is a contract between the purchaser and the insurance company. The purchaser or policyholder gives money (either in a lump sum or over time) to an insurance company for a guaranteed return.

Annuities come in lots of flavors:

- Fixed: A fixed annuity comes with a guaranteed return (say 5 percent) if held to maturity. Fixed annuities are long-term, tax-deferred insurance contracts designed for retirement. It allows you to create a fixed stream of income through a process called annuitization and also provides a fixed rate of return based on the terms of the contract. Fixed annuities have limitations. If you decide to take your money out early, you may face fees called surrender charges. Plus, if you're not yet 59 1/2, you may also have to pay an additional 10% tax penalty on top of ordinary income taxes. You should also know that a fixed annuity contains guarantees and protections that are subject to the issuing insurance company's ability to pay for them.

- Deferred or immediate: A deferred annuity has a time in the future when the policyholder will expect the insurance company to make good on its guarantees, whereas an immediate annuity generally initializes the guarantee within the first thirty days.

- Indexed annuities: A type of fixed annuity that has a value tied to various market indices.

- Riders: Most annuities have riders attached to the insurance product that the policyholder can choose to add—or not. These riders all carry fees determined by actuarial estimates. Examples include enhanced death benefits, income payouts for life, beneficiary payouts for life, nursing-home care.

Unfortunately, many people think annuities have a negative connotation. They are complicated products that often are sold by less-than-scrupulous salespeople. Clients often tell me about relatives and friends who were sold annuities that carried large fees or had a long-term surrender that was not appropriate to the buyer. Some of my clients refuse to have annuities, a request that I honor, of course. However, I always tell people that an annuity is just like a car: there are good ones, and there are bad ones. When purchasing an annuity, you need to make sure that you understand everything beforehand.

I see annuities as a way to give you the guarantee of income that you might have with a pension. If you have a pension when you retire, it's wonderful. However, there's always the chance it might not last. And if you do not have a pension to fall back on, we strive to create one for you by buying an annuity through an insurance company. They can be especially important instruments for an Income Tomorrow portfolio as they have income streams that can be turned on and off and they can guarantee that you will not outlive them.

Guarantees are based on the claims paying ability of the insurance company.

ADJUSTABLE INCOME STREAM

The details can seem like a lot, but essentially, annuities have two phases: the accumulation phase and the income-stream payout. You can elect when to turn on that income stream, which is a feature that gives us some flexibility. You might elect to use your Income Tomorrow for an income stream when you retire and let your Social Security grow until you are sixty-seven or seventy. You might instead decide not to turn on that income stream when you retire and instead live off your Income Today, leaving Income Tomorrow for a backup plan.

For example, a client might put $180,000 in an annuity in Income Tomorrow. This client may want to purchase an expensive item, but did not have enough money to do so. The client could start an income stream on the Income Tomorrow part of her portfolio. In essence, her Income Tomorrow is designed to be a self-pension that she can use however she wants.

LIVING-BENEFIT FEATURE

Many annuities will guarantee that you will not outlive them—a feature called a "living benefit," for which you pay about 1 percent. If you pass away, the same amount of money will continue to be paid to your designated survivor. And if you also have a joint-life payout, whatever value is left when you pass away goes to your beneficiaries. In this way an annuity can be better than a pension. When the recipient of the pension dies, that's it. The spouse or children may not get anything.

The living-benefit feature is basically an insurance policy on a nest egg. Paying, say, $2,000 for insurance on your $200,000 nest egg in the annuity may be a wise idea. After all, you may pay $2,000 for the insurance on your house so that you will be covered in case the house burns down, and you may pay $2,000 a year for car insurance in case your car is in an accident. Bad things do happen, and it's important to be covered.

THE DOWNSIDE OF ANNUITIES

A wise buyer is an informed buyer when it comes to annuities. They can have surrender fees, which are fees you must pay if you decide you would like to get all your money back before a certain date. I will not sell an annuity with a surrender fee longer than seven years. My reasoning is common sense: according to the US Census Bureau (as updated in their May 2011 publication), marriages that end in divorce last for a median of eight years for both men and women. So why should we have to stay married to a product for more than seven years? Anything over ten years is definitely unacceptable. A ninety-year-old client came to me with an annuity she bought when she was eighty-five. It has a seventeen-year surrender charge. I consider that unethical.

Another thing to consider in buying an annuity is the terms of its joint-life payout. Be sure to find out if the annuity can have contingent beneficiaries if your primary beneficiary passes away before you. Other items for buyers to consider should include the cost and length of any early withdrawal penalties as well as tax ramifications at the time of annuity distributions.

Another complaint about annuities is that they are expensive—most are about 3 percent. However, it's like putting your money in a bank. The bank is loaning out your money at 6 percent and giving you 0–1 percent at the most. The bank is certainly making money on your money. But for whatever reason, some people object more

Guarantees are based on the claims paying ability of the insurance company.

when it's packaged in an annuity. Keep in mind that an annuity is insurance. Think about it: we might pay a lot more than 3 percent of the value of our car on car insurance if that car is old. The value of my teenager's car is $500, and the insurance premiums are $1,000. Granted, it is terrifying to give an insurance company $200,000, basically hoping that the company is going to be there until you die and is going to continue to pay out your benefits. But that is true of all pensions. This is why annuities are just one piece of your portfolio plan.

BONDS AS AN ALTERNATIVE

Another type of investment we might consider for Income Tomorrow is an insured and guaranteed bond.

You used to be able to buy a $100,000 bond that would pay 5 percent, or $5,000, for the next twenty years. And at the end of that twenty years, you would get your $100,000 back. That was secure, and it certainly would meet our guarantee for the Income Tomorrow piece. The problem is that there are no such things as high-quality 5 percent bonds at the current time. With a guaranteed bond, your monthly check will be steady, and inflation will eat into the value of that check year after year.

If a bond is listed as "insured," the insurance relates only to the prompt payment of principal and interest of the securities in the portfolio. This does not remove market risk. Yield and market value will fluctuate with changes in market conditions. Price and availability are subject to change without notice. Investing involves risk and investors may incur a profit or a loss.

INCOME TOMORROW: AN EXAMPLE

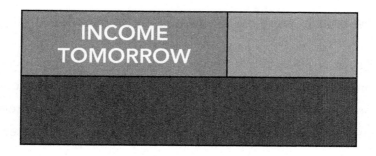

The graphic shows the Income Tomorrow piece of the same theoretical portfolio described in chapter 3.

Using Clara Client as an example again, she chose an annuity with a living benefit rider and a "roll up" guarantee during the accumulation phase (when Clara wasn't taking any distributions). So when we put in $200,000, we know that in twelve years, or December 1, 2027, that $200,000 will be $400,000 (through the utilization of a guaranteed income product) for income purposes. We are going to take 5 percent of it, or $20,000, to start another income stream. Remember from chapter 3 that Clara has $1,628 coming from the dividends and interest in the Income Today piece every month, as well as Social Security.

CLARA CLIENT PIECE BY PIECE PLAN ™

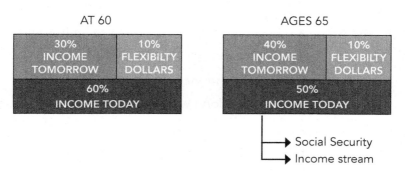

QUESTION AND ANSWER

Where can I find more information on annuities?

There are many types of annuities. At a minimum, there are fixed annuities, equity-indexed annuities, variable annuities, single-premium annuities, and tax-deferred annuities. Other terminology includes participation rates, cap rates, income base, accumulation phase, distribution phase, annuitization, surrender schedules, riders, death benefits, enhanced death benefits, and on and on. Annuities are very complex products and should not be entered into without much consideration. As an investor, keep asking questions until you're convinced that you understand what you're getting and the commensurate cost.

What about required minimum distributions?

Every client and advisor definitely needs to make sure that all of the regulations are followed for RMDs. If an annuity contract has been funded with qualified dollars (IRAs, 401(k)s, etc.), then the 12/31 balance from the prior year needs to be considered along with any IRAs, etc. The correct life expectancy factor (LEF) needs to be utilized (in IRS and tax publications) as well. The penalty for not taking the minimum amount is the income tax owed plus a 50 percent excise tax. So we don't want to get this wrong! Tax preparers, advisors, and clients all need to work closely to make sure that all computations are done correctly.

CHAPTER 5

FLEXIBILITY DOLLARS: BECAUSE STUFF HAPPENS

The Flexibility Dollars piece of the Piece by Piece™ plan is designed to allow you to roll with the punches after you retire. It gives you flexibility to cover the unexpected expenses we all have now and then. This is money for immediate use in emergencies or unexpected needs, such as weddings, new roofs, and huge car repair bills. Your children may run into a temporary roadblock and you want to help. Or you might have a health issue and need extra money to pay some of the medical bills and do rehab in a nicer facility. One of my clients, a builder, decided to use his Flexibility Dollars account when he was diagnosed with multiple sclerosis. He had been working half time, but once he got sick he retired completely. He decided to pull half of his Flexibility Dollars money to plan some trips before he got so sick that he could not travel easily.

I normally allocate 10–15 percent of the money from a client's nest egg for Flexibility Dollars. The investments in this piece must be very liquid because when you need the money, you need it *now*.

This part of the plan is, as its name implies, very flexible. Therefore, I make sure that clients understand what their decisions mean when they decide to spend funds in this piece. They decide for themselves *when* they want to spend their Flexibility Dollars money, *if* they want to spend their Flexibility Dollars, and if they need to increase their Flexibility Dollars. (Personally, I like to have a lot in my Flexibility Dollars account because I don't like to live on the edge.)

Roth IRAs are usually part of my client's Flexibility Dollars. Because Roths were created fairly recently, many people have not yet utilized them. Some people may make too much money; they are over the modified adjusted gross income (MAGI) amount in order to make a contribution. Others may make too little money to contribute to a Roth, as they must defer enough income inside their company plan in order to receive their employer's matching dollars. Qualified Roth distributions are tax-free*. This can be a wonderful bonus for Flexibility Dollars! It can allow a client access to these funds for an unanticipated need that won't affect his or her tax planning.

---

*Unless certain criteria are met, Roth IRA owners must be 59 1/2 or older and have held the IRA for five years before tax-free withdrawals are permitted.

IT'S YOUR CHOICE . . . FOR LIFE

How much you put in your Flexibility Dollars piece and how you use those funds are up to you. Some people feel they need less flexibility when a spouse is still working part-time. In contrast, one of my clients, who I'll call Nathan, absolutely refused to have funds in the Income Tomorrow backup plan. He wanted to put 90 percent of what would have been in that backup plan into Flexibility Dollars and the remaining 10 percent into Income Today. Nathan felt that his pension was his backup plan—his fallback money—and that if he needed more flexibility later, he could use his Flexibility Dollars.

Very early in my financial-planning career I put together a customized plan for a client whose husband had just passed away. Beth had sold their printing business and had good sums in Income Today and Income Tomorrow. I was even able to put $90,000 in her Flexibility Dollars piece. Within two weeks, however, she had called me to liquidate the $90,000 so she could buy a condominium and move close to her daughter and a disabled grandchild.

I said, "We just had this discussion! You were not going to make any decisions during the first year after your husband passed away. You do realize that now you aren't going to have any flexibility left, so if something comes up, you will only have Income Today for your check and Income Tomorrow for your backup plan." I was particularly concerned because Beth was only fifty-eight.

She insisted: She was going to empty her Flexibility Dollars piece. And that's exactly what she did. She knew that the money was there, that it was the flexible piece, and she decided she was going to use all of it so she could move. She knew that using it would not affect her Income Today or her Income Tomorrow; she would potentially still have that money to live on. And, of course, she also realized it would mean she would be out of Flexibility Dollars for life. Some people like to live life a little more on the financial edge than others.

BETH'S PIECE BY PIECE™ PLAN

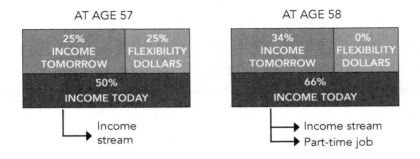

She understood the ramifications of the decision she was making at the time she made it. I'm happy to let my clients make the decision that is right for them after discussing the pros and cons of the longer term potential outcomes.

THOSE "EXPECTED" UNEXPECTED EMERGENCIES

Propane rates here in northern Michigan were really high in 2014. People were shocked at how much they had to spend to fill their tank in the fall—and then that fall was followed by a very cold, snowy winter. Some of my clients had propane bills that were about three times normal. It was just one of those years. (The next year it was fifty-nine degrees in December, and we had little snow.)

To cover their unexpectedly high fuel bills, my clients had a choice: pay the bills from their monthly paycheck and lower their standard of living during that time *or* use some of their Flexibility Dollars. Using Income Tomorrow was not a good option; we did not want to ruin any future guarantees on annuities. Flexibility Dollars are designed to be used in cases like this, when you need some extra money for those expenses that just tend to come up in life.

FLEXIBILITY FOR THE GOOD STUFF

The Flexibility Dollars piece of your retirement plan can be larger or smaller at different times, depending on what is going on in your life at that particular time. Francis and Monica, clients of mine, had an initial retirement plan that was pretty normal: 65 percent in Income Today, 25 percent in Income Tomorrow, and 10 percent in Flexibility Dollars. Unexpectedly, they came into a large inheritance. They decided to put 50 percent of their nest egg in Flexibility Dollars so that they could easily gift $5,000 per child to their grandchildren's college accounts every Christmas. They also support missionary work in Hungary out of their Flexibility Dollars. Due to the additional dollars provided by the inheritance, Francis and Monica ultimately had a Piece by Piece™ plan that allocated 35 percent to Income Today, 15 percent to Income Tomorrow, and 50 percent to Flexibility Dollars.

WHAT TO AVOID DOING WITH THOSE FLEXIBILITY DOLLARS

Jane, another client, also inherited a lot of money. As sometimes happens in such circumstances, people in the family began to call and ask her for money. She began to gift $5,000 here and $10,000 there to help out relatives. They knew she had a good heart, and some of them took advantage of her.

After almost a year, I had to have a talk with her: "This is your money, and you can do whatever you want to do with it. But next time, instead of saying yes right away when someone calls and asks you for money, please say, 'I want to do this for you, but you have to call my financial advisor first.'" My goal is to protect the interest of my clients and help achieve an outcome that is in their best interest.

INVESTMENTS IN FLEXIBILITY DOLLARS

I choose investments in the Flexibility Dollars part of the portfolio very conservatively. The balance needs to be fairly steady, and the funds need to be liquid so that when people need the money, there is a greater potential for it to be available. It might be two years down the road, or it might be eight years. They might need 10 percent of it, or they might need all of it. Who knows?

I strive to achieve these goals by recommending three or four different investments with *low correlation*—meaning they rarely move in the same direction. That way, when we need funds, one of those investments may have performed positively and made money, and we can potentially utilize it at that time. If there's a disaster in one sector of the economy, we may have only lost a relatively small amount. Hopefully, this performance is not going to hurt our overall portfolio.

Say a client has $50,000 in the Flexibility Dollars piece of the plan, I may put $12,500 in four different investments that I think are going to move in different directions. I might select investments involving gold, metals, or other commodities because they move differently than the market does. Second, I may utilize an investment in biotechnology or science—areas that depend on innovation and may be more growth-oriented. Third, I may choose an investment that is considered as total-return so it is designed to be more balanced in how it performs. A total-return or balanced investment tends to take on less market volatility by choosing blue chip stocks and bonds. Finally, I usually elect to use a floating-rate investment because it is designed to be less volatile. Floating-rate investments are "low duration"—typically bonds that are sixty days to twenty-four months—so they aren't usually subjected to the price volatility that can occur when interest rates change.

FLEXIBILITY DOLLARS: A CLARA CLIENT EXAMPLE

Clara Client had a Roth IRA. Since she would be working for another five years, her Roth IRA became part of her Flexibility Dollars piece.

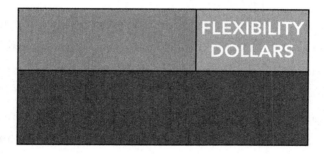

In addition to Clara's $40,000 Roth IRA, she has an extra savings account with a balance of $15,000. We utilized these two investments (Roth and savings) to start Clara's Flexibility Dollar piece in our preretirement meeting. For the rest of the investments in Flexibility Dollars, I picked three different things (investing $5,000 in each) that very rarely move in the same direction at the same time. I don't know which one of them will be better, but one of them will have outperformed the other two.

Commodities and currencies investing are generally considered speculative because of the significant potential for investment loss. Their markets are likely to be volatile and there may be sharp price fluctuations even during periods when prices overall are rising. Keep in mind that there is no assurance that any strategy will ultimately be successful or profitable nor protect against a loss.

Clara's Flexibility Dollars were invested equally in:

- a total-return/balanced investment

- an alternative-investment

- a municipal bond investment

A total-return/balanced investment is designed to have moderate risk with holdings balanced between stocks, bonds, international equities, or Treasury notes for diversification. An alternative-investment will typically invest in commodities, emerging market equities or debt, currency, real estate, etc.

A municipal bond investment will generally provide tax-free income to the client by investing in a portfolio of municipal bonds. These bonds are usually loans to municipalities for building schools, roads, hospitals, etc.

Additional options might include the common stocks of companies that hold an interest to the client, laddered CDs, or other alternatives. I'm ready if Clara comes to me and says, "I need $5,000, and I need it in three days." Having this Flexibility Dollars piece allows me to say, "Okay, from which of these four items would you like to sell $5,000?" This is a very good time to have a tax advisor that is part of the advisor/client team. When determining which investment to liquidate to get the needed $5,000, taxes need to be considered. In a year with higher than normal income, perhaps the client's tax advisor would recommend selling an investment which has experienced a loss, enabling the client to "harvest" the loss for tax purposes.

Income from municipal bonds is not subject to federal income taxation; however, it may be subject to state and local taxes and, for certain investors, to the alternative minimum tax. Income from taxable municipal bonds is subject to federal income taxation, and it may be subject to state and local taxes. Investing involves risk and you may incur a profit or loss regardless of strategy selected. This is a hypothetical example and individual investor's results will vary.

In a year when the client had lower than normal earnings, the tax advisor might recommend selling an investment at a profit and paying capital gains taxes. Or perhaps the better decision is taking $5,000 from the client's Roth. The team approach to financial planning is usually in the client's best interest.

You will recall from chapter 3 that Fred and Rita were expecting an inheritance and thus decided to reinvest all the Income Today earnings the first year rather than use them for a monthly paycheck. Instead, they decided to take those paychecks out of the Flexibility Dollars. They would use the cash portion for twelve months or about $32,000–$35,000 of it. That would leave $15,000 in cash after that first year. When they got their inheritance, they would put the money back in Flexibility Dollars to bring it back up to $50,000 in cash.

Flexibility dollars are designed to operate like a portfolio's "pressure relief valve." Life tends to be filled with events that can't be planned for. Most clients would prefer not to lower their monthly retirement check by having to sell the Income Today investments. Similarly, they would prefer not to reduce any guarantees from the insurance company annuities for Income Tomorrow. One of the goals of the Piece by Piece™ plan is to help my clients feel confident going into retirement; the choices afforded by flexibility dollars are there to assist.

QUESTION AND ANSWER

What about using flexibility dollars for long-term care?

Flexibility dollars are part of the Piece by Piece™ plan to provide for anything that might be a concern in retirement that wasn't considered in the original retirement plan. It might be moving expenses, a second home, health-care premiums prior to Medicare, family vacations, long-term care, grandkids' college, charitable gifting, or even bail money! (We probably wouldn't have considered needing that last one!)

How should I categorize an inheritance for retirement-income planning purposes?

As a wonderful blessing! Inheritances are generally not planned for; they just happen to us. One woman I work with used an inheritance from her mother to fund fifteen years of family vacations with her three children, their spouses, and eight grandchildren. A single gentleman funded his long-term-care expenses. Another client supports Hungarian missionaries and planting churches. Yet another paid for grandchildren's college tuition bills. Inheritances can fill a void in a retirement plan or be used outside of the plan for legacy purposes.

CHAPTER 6

A RETIREMENT PLAN JUST FOR YOU . . . LET'S GET STARTED!

I n retirement, we obviously want our investments to generate income for us—to pay out money every month in the form of a "retirement check." However, we never know how long we will live, so we also need our investments to have a growth component. In other words, our investment portfolio must continue to generate income for us no matter how long we live.

Retirement-income planning is challenging because everyone is different. Situations vary, and we all differ in how we feel about money and about risk. And even with careful planning, unexpected things happens. A grandchild gets sick, a child plans a destination wedding, or the car needs a new transmission.

It would be great if there was a generic retirement-income plan that would fit everybody, but it never really works out that way. Financial-planning software does not take our individuality into account. It takes our numbers, puts them in the black box, and tells us what we will get every month. I believe approaches like systematic withdrawal have no flexibility, either.

I know it's very hard to find that one financial advisor you really trust; it's difficult to get financially naked and lay out your needs and resources in front of someone, but that is really what you need to do. You want to find that person you can trust to help you get all your ducks in a row so that you can be confident—both before and after you retire.

As a financial advisor, I work very hard to create a Piece by Piece™ plan customized to help you to have an enriching retirement. I want you to be able to do the kinds of things you have dreamed about and remain confident when unforeseen circumstances arise. When I create your plan, I am careful to help you understand what I am doing and why I am doing it. I call you before I make any changes. It may be confusing at first, but I try to persist, and after a while, hopefully, my clients feel good that they understand their plans; I want them to feel in charge of their finances. If we never discussed the details, you'd always be just hoping things worked out. I want you to *feel confident* . . . every step of the way.

Before our first meeting, I will send you a questionnaire and a list of what I'd like you to bring in to our first meeting. Then we'll sit down and talk about your goals in retirement, what you have to work with, and how we can make it work for you.

Keep in mind that there is no assurance that any strategy will ultimately be successful or profitable nor protect against a loss.

HOW MUCH DO YOU WANT TO LIVE ON EACH MONTH?

One of the first things we do when we meet is determine *The Number*: how much money you will need each month when you retire.

Many planners start by asking, "How much do you live on each month?" or saying, "Bring in your budget, and we'll go over it." I have never had a person come into my office and announce that they need to live on, say, $5,000 a month—not one. It is really hard to say how much you will need for retirement. You may be one of those few people who are actually comfortable looking at their expenses— "I spend this much on window washing and this much on lawn mowing and this much on my insurance, utilities, and those kinds of things"—and then adding up their budget. Most people, though, have no idea how much money they need to live on, and creating budgets is very difficult—mostly because people don't perceive it to be any fun!

Some financial advisors base your monthly paycheck on what is called a *replacement ratio*. You choose a certain percentage of your current income to be replaced in retirement—most commonly 60 percent to 80 percent. So if you make $100,000 and you want an 80 percent replacement ratio, then you'll want to find a way to make $80,000 a year in retirement. The thinking is that some of your income will be replaced by Social Security and that your tax bracket will be lower.

Even that seems too arbitrary to me, so I usually advise clients to base their monthly check during retirement on their paycheck before retirement. I generally begin by asking, "If I were able to give you the same amount of money you are making today, would that be okay?" People like to think that they actually earn the *gross* amount on their check each week. It makes us feel better for all of that work we are putting in! But we really live on the *net* amount.

So we start with your gross amount, then subtract FICA taxes and the retirement contribution. This amount is higher than the actual net amount at the bottom of your pay stub, so it potentially increases your comfort level with the Piece by Piece™ plan.

Once we know that number, we find a way to help generate enough income for today, for tomorrow in case something happens, and then some flexibility. My goal is to get the same amount that you now take home after FICA (Social Security and Medicare) deductions and your 401(k) or other retirement contributions. You do not see that money anyway, so you may be able to live without it in your retirement checks as well. After all, you are figuring out a way to make it work *right now*, so you may figure out a way to make that same amount work *in retirement*.

Then, using the number we determine would be your monthly paycheck, we establish what your nest egg needs to look like. In other words, if you need to live on $50,000 a year, how much do you need to have today to have $50,000 each year until you die?

This is why I feel it's best to begin this process ten years before you plan to retire: you may have the potential to build up your nest egg for us to work with once you retire. Five years before you retire still gives us some time to potentially build up your nest egg. Unfortunately, though, some people seek financial planning help the month before they want to retire, when the amount of money in that nest egg is as large as it's going to be. We can still work with this situation, but it is far better to plan ahead.

WHAT SIZE IS YOUR NEST EGG? OR WHERE DID I LEAVE THAT MONEY?

Once we know the target for your monthly paycheck, we have a discovery meeting to determine all the assets you have that we can use for retirement—the size of your nest egg. We look at balances in current retirement plans, old employer plans, brokerage accounts, banks, pensions, and ex-spouse benefits.

We go through the questionnaire about your finances that I sent you prior to the meeting. It includes questions on whether you have any pensions, whether you worked anywhere other than the source of that pension for ten years (in case you might have a pension there), what your Social Security estimates are, whether you have any inheritances, how old you are (which determines how long we have to put things in place prior to Social Security starting), and whether you or your spouse has a 401(k), an IRA, or a 403(b) type of retirement plan.

We also determine whether the money from the various sources is available to be moved around. Sometimes assets cannot be used for retirement, such as Roth IRAs that are earmarked for grandkids' college education or legacies. We talk about whether you want to use all the money that is available in these plans during your retirement so that the day you breathe your last breath is the day you spend your last dime. Or, instead, whether you might want to leave some of your money to your children, the church, or a charity of your choice.

Everybody has a different answer; no two people have ever told me the same thing. Some say, "I'll never live ten years. My brother and sister died young, so I probably will, too." Others have parents in their late nineties—so they believe they will live a very long time after retirement and expect that their money will have to last a long time, too.

We also determine when you want to retire. Are you planning ahead ten years? Are you trying to retire in six months or in six days? Or, did you retire last year, live on your savings for a year, and now need to start a plan? Again, I have to admit that most people do not plan ahead ten or even five years, when we could work with the money and allow it to potentially grow. Generally, we have to work with what we have. We sit down at the table and try to figure out how we can get the most out of that nest egg.

SOCIAL SECURITY—WHAT DOES IT MEAN FOR YOU?

One of the first things we do to get a picture of your future income is look at your Social Security estimated benefits. Every year, sixty days before your birthday, you will have been receiving in the mail a notice that explains your benefits. You also can go online and get this statement at SSA.gov. It will show you your up-to-date estimates and different strategies you might choose for using your benefits.

You can start getting Social Security at age sixty-two to sixty-five or at your full retirement age—which depends on the year you were born but is probably sixty-six or sixty-six and some-odd months or sixty-seven. If you delay retirement beyond your full retirement age, waiting until you are seventy, you will actually get an 8 percent increase every year from the time of your full retirement.

If you and your spouse are both eligible for Social Security benefits, you might use one of several strategies. For example, you might decide to claim one person's benefits first and use the spousal benefits on that one. These decisions are important and have long-term effects, so we will talk through them in detail.

DECIDING WHEN TO RETIRE

Social Security benefits are determined using a worker's total yearly earnings to figure your Social Security credits. The amount needed for a credit in 2016 is $1,260 (adjusted annually when average wages increase). Workers can earn a maximum of four credits for any year. For most workers, their final years are their highest earning years. These higher "credits" replace lower ones in the benefit calculation. There can be a tendency to set a retirement date of 12/31 ensuring their highest annual pay, however, there are other considerations. I tell them that, instead, they should "retire at a time when it's light out when you wake up and light out nearly until you go to bed."

Especially in cold climates, I believe retiring on December 31 is not the best idea. The holidays are over, and you and your significant other are sitting there in the living room, looking at each other, and wondering what to do: "I won't get dressed today, because I probably won't have to go out. It's not like I need to mow the lawn or anything." In the summer, though, it's nice outside, and there are a million things to do. My clients here in Michigan tend to do better when they retire in April or May. And then they will have been retired for a while before winter comes along; they may have established a schedule or rhythm that allows them to enjoy themselves and get on with life.

Remember that any change—even a good change—is one of the most stressful things there is. So if you add in the dark and dreary days of winter and suddenly being together with your spouse all day, every day, it can be a challenging transition. Instead, consider retiring in the spring.

PENSIONS: YOU MAY HAVE MORE THAN YOU REALIZE

It may be hard to believe, but people often are unaware that they have a pension or, if they do, what its terms are. Many people have a number of retirement plans in different places, and it can be easy to lose track of where all that money is. If you have money in a 401(k) pension plan from a former employer, you should get a yearly statement. However, you can't count on it; your employer may have lost track of you and stopped sending those notices. You may have been vested thirty years ago and moved around a lot. If you are nodding your head in recognition, you are not alone. It is very common for people to come to me without knowing where their money is, how much it totals, and when they can access it. Wealthy people, poor people, smart people . . . it's true across the board. We go on to our next job and tend to of forget about it. And then we move, and our mail is only forwarded for a year—and then it is gone from our mailboxes and our minds.

One man, Mitchell, came to my office last week and learned why we call it a "discovery" meeting: He found that he had a pension he had not even realized he had. He had worked for a company when he was in his twenties and had paid little attention to it back then. (We all feel we're invincible at that age!) He said to me, "You know, they kept sending me this stuff once a year, and I would just throw it in a pile. I finally opened one of the mailings because it said, 'Final notice.'" Mitch realized that the mailing was informing him about an old pension with a benefit to which he was entitled.

It is also not at all uncommon for people to misunderstand how they can use money in their various pension funds. A woman and I were starting the discovery process, and she revealed that she had a hospital pension in another state but was not able to move it. I said, "Let's find out how much that pension benefit is going to be at age sixty. It does not matter if you can move it or cannot move it. The important thing is knowing that it is there and that we know how much of a benefit it will be when you hit a certain age."

So in our discovery meeting—which, again, is obviously well named—we brainstorm. I ask, "Who are your former employers? How much money do you currently have in 401(k) plans? In banks? In brokerage accounts? (A brokerage account is similar to a bank account, but instead of the funds being held at a bank, they are held at a brokerage house.) Do you have any old credit union accounts that you have forgotten about? When I was first married I left five dollars in a credit union in Lansing because I could get cheaper auto loans there. I moved a long time ago and forgot about it. When I finally remembered, it was only worth about $10, but I had them mail me a check and closed the account.

UNCLAIMED PROPERTY LIST: ANOTHER POSSIBLE SOURCE OF INCOME

One way you might find out about assets you have forgotten about is through the unclaimed-property list compiled by each state. Maybe you had a bank account in town when you went to college years ago. Or you had a $100 lab fee that you never got back for a class you never took after you dropped out. You have moved since then, so even if they had sent you a notice, you would never have received it. By law, every financial institution has to send a notice of such unclaimed property to the state every year.

You can go online and look at the list. Once you prove your identity, you will be sent your money. Many people don't know that the unclaimed-property list exists, but it's worth a look to see if you have anything there.

CONSOLIDATING FUNDS

Once we have brought together an accurate and up-to-date picture of your nest egg, we generally consolidate all the sources of income. Having your funds in one place allows us to take a holistic look at what we have to work with, as well as to do a gap analysis on what we are missing. By reducing multiple accounts, it also allows us to help diversify your investments and potentially reduce fees. And should something happen to you, your beneficiaries may find it much easier if your money is not spread out over multiple accounts across the country.

FINANCIAL BENEFITS OF CONSOLIDATION

Many people are aware that diversification can potentially reduce volatility, and having a holistic picture of your nest egg helps us achieve that diversification. I began working with one of my clients, a dentist, about twelve years ago. She brought me her statements from seven different accounts. When I asked why she had seven accounts, she said, "Because they are diversified. I don't want to have all my eggs in one basket." I asked, "How do you know they are diversified?" We looked into it, and it turned out that she owned health care investments in all seven accounts. She was a dentist, so health care was what she knew. Generally, my goal is to put my client's assets together to be appropriately allocated and diversified.

The key is to remember that just because your assets are in seven places does *not* mean they are diversified. Consolidating accounts is a good way to help achieve diversification. Having just one account can potentially help cut down on fees. After all, if you have seven accounts, you are paying seven account fees. Some kinds of plans, such as Roth IRAs, also offer more appropriate tax incentives than others.

Diversification does not ensure a profit or guarantee against a loss. Keep in mind that there is no assurance that any strategy will ultimately be successful or profitable nor protect against a loss.

VERIFYING BENEFICIARIES

Consolidation allows you to revisit your decisions on beneficiaries and make sure they conform to your current wishes. When you were at Employer A fifteen years ago, you may have had a spouse and one child listed as beneficiaries of your pension plan. Then you divorced, married again, and had two more children. Do you even remember whether your pension plans and 401(k)s since that time include all three children as your beneficiaries? You will want to make sure that the beneficiaries named in your plans are who you actually *want* them to be.

Another thing to think about is whether your beneficiaries would know where you have worked in the past if they needed to access the accounts. Most people today have worked for at least three or four different places by the time they are even fifty or fifty-five, and many have ignored all those 401(k) plans from former employers.

I encourage everyone to consider consolidating their retirement plans. That way, if you become disabled or die, your spouse or other beneficiaries will be able to access them more easily. In addition, if you have accounts in fifteen different places, it is almost impossible to make sure that your wishes for all fifteen of those accounts stay up to date.

It is important to remember that if you die, the beneficiary named on the account is going to get the money. There's no fixing it. I talked to a client who had just had his sixth child, and he admitted that he and his wife were glad they had thought to do the paperwork to add that child to their beneficiaries list.

Another client wanted to retire early and take an early-out package; he was sixty. When he was forty, he got divorced and had a qualified domestic relations order (QDRO) that said that his wife at the time (now his ex-wife) would get 50 percent of his pension. That is fairly typical. Now time had passed. As part of the early-retirement plan, he had the opportunity to take a lump-sum distribution instead of taking a pension. We talked it over and figured out that the pension is $500 a month, but if he takes the lump sum, we might be able to generate an income of $600 a month. Obviously, he wants to take the lump sum. But the QDRO on this pension basically says, "We're not going to send you the lump sum until your ex-spouse signs off on it." My client had to go back to the attorney who had done his divorce twenty years earlier so he could act on his pension.

Beneficiaries count! You can't leave any of this to chance. Another client had an ex-wife and two children with her as well as a longtime girlfriend and a child with her. The client listed his ex-wife as the only beneficiary. Every year when we reviewed his plan, I would say, "Your ex-wife is still the beneficiary." He would say, "I know, but nothing is going to happen to me, and if it does, my ex-wife will make sure that the money goes to all the kids. She'll do the right thing."

I said, "You know, even Mother Teresa might have a hard time doing the right thing in this situation; one person is going to get the money, and I really don't think she is going to want to divide it three ways. Even if she does not take it herself, she probably will give it to her two children, as opposed to all three of your children." My client would think hard about it every year because it's really tough to make that call, but then he would say, "No, it's fine."

I'm afraid you can see where this is going. He died when he was out of town on business. He had only been gone two days when his ex-wife came into my office, saying, "I understand that I am the beneficiary of his IRA." I said, "That's true. We'll go get the death certificate and start the process. But I do want to tell you that you can disclaim the benefit. This means you can change the benefit and divide it between your ex-husband's three kids." I wanted her to know that it was not too late to divide the money differently than in the paperwork. She looked me straight in the eye and said, "This is mine, and he wanted me to have it." Of course, I prepared the paperwork accordingly.

Sometimes a client wants to name their oldest child of several as a beneficiary and then let that person divide up the money among the siblings. This is not a good idea. It puts a tremendous burden on that individual, who then also gets all the tax liability. Be sure to clarify your precise wishes from the beginning.

PUTTING THE PIECES TOGETHER: DESIGNING YOUR PERSONALIZED PLAN

By this point in the process, we will have talked about how much money you want to generate as income in retirement. We will have looked at what you have—your current balances plus all your old retirement plans, as well as what you can expect from your Social Security benefits when you retire.

You want to hit retirement with everything in place. Again, the earlier you begin planning for your retirement income, the better. I believe ten years is ideal, though five years may still give us some time to put things in place. This discussion assumes you begin working with me in that time frame. If not, though, there are still things we can do.

USING THE GAP YEARS WISELY

Let's assume that you have determined that you would like to retire on $50,000 a year. You may get $20,000 from Social Security, and you know the balance in your nest egg. Next, we determine whether that amount will generate the income you will need to fill in that $30,000 gap. Or will we need to do something in the next five to seven years until you retire to bring up that balance? If so, we'll look at that gap together and decide an appropriate approach for attempting to fill it.

We have many choices, and I will ask you lots of questions to figure out an appropriate approach. Are you in a high-income tax bracket and might need to look at a tax-deferred plan like an IRA or 401(k) so that you won't have to pay taxes on it until you retire? Are you able to utilize your employer retirement plan? Does your employer pay a match into a retirement fund? And, if so, are you taking advantage of it?

Maybe even a regular old savings account or an old-fashioned investment account would be your choice in case you might need to access that money. I always call such vehicles "savings without handcuffs"—because they lack the restrictions of vehicles like 401(k) or IRA plans, which tell you how long you have to leave the funds in the plan, the age you have to be when you take them out, or the kinds of investments that must be inside.

When we're filling the gap, we strive to use the most appropriate or most advantageous vehicle or product for our target retirement date. We create a plan designed to fill in the gap so that when you hit that time down the road when you want to retire, you will potentially be able to generate your Income Today. We also want you to be at the point where your backup plan (Income Tomorrow) is ready in case *that* needs to be started up. Plus we want to have your Flexibility Dollars in place.

Your plan will be designed to give you confidence through market volatility and will potentially help you retire in a few years ready to kayak, travel, or enjoy other pursuits.

HEALTH CARE AFTER RETIREMENT

Health-care costs are an important consideration if you retire before you are eligible for Medicare. COBRA costs about $1,800 a month.[2] And as I've noted, a couple would typically pay $1,200 to $1,500 a month for their combined health care before Medicare—and that is for a plan with extremely high deductibles and out-of-pocket expenses.

For anyone considering a retirement date prior to receiving Medicare benefits, a plan needs to be in place for paying the high cost of health insurance. Some young retirees will choose to withdraw

---

2 According to the Dept. of Labor website: "The Consolidated Omnibus Budget Reconciliation Act (COBRA) gives workers and their families who lose their health benefits the right to choose to continue group health benefits provided by their group health plan for limited periods of time under certain circumstances such as voluntary or involuntary job loss, reduction in the hours worked, transition between jobs, death, divorce, and other life events. COBRA outlines how employees and family members may elect continuation coverage."
Keep in mind that there is no assurance that any strategy will ultimately be successful or profitable nor protect against a loss.

10–12 percent from their Income Today piece instead of the recommended 4–5 percent. Once his or her Medicare benefits begin, the retiree can potentially reduce those distributions to 3–4 percent in order to allow some potential growth and reinvestment in their Income Today piece of their retirement plan.

Other people decide to work part time to pay for health care until Medicare kicks in. In that case, it may be beneficial to put money in a Roth IRA because of the lower tax bracket. If you decide to work part time for your health benefits, keep in mind that there could be a catch-22. If your health declines and you can no longer work, it could be problematic. Therefore, don't count on being able to work part time or do side jobs in your retirement. It's best to have a plan designed to work no matter what your health turns out to be.

Every person—and every plan—is completely different. In some professions, former workers can elect to work one week a quarter and get paid quite well or get health-care benefits. One example would be retired utility company employees who add their name to lists for future dispatch for storm duty. Another option is a company that allows certain employees to retire and then come back to work on special projects as "contract" workers or consultants. Other people decide to work until their full retirement age (FRA) for full Social Security benefits. The earlier an employee can start considering the options and planning for retirement, the more choices may be available as their retirement date gets closer.

PLANNING THOSE WONDERFUL RETIREMENT YEARS

The goal of the Piece by Piece™ plan is to allow you to never see a difference in your monthly paycheck after you retire—no matter how long you live.

In planning your portfolio, I keep in mind that retirement generally looks different at the beginning and at the end, and your portfolio will, too. Of course, this progression happens at a different pace for everybody, but three phases are typical.

Within the financial-planning industry, we call the first ten years the go-go years. You are on the go—golfing, seeing grandkids, and doing a lot of traveling while healthy and fit. You tend to spend money on things that make you happy. Next are the middle years, the slow-go years. At this time you might contemplate a trip to Hawaii but think, *It's such a long flight, and my back gets so sore. Maybe we'll stay closer to home.* Finally are the no-go years—basically your Drew Carey years, when you just stay home and watch *The Price is Right.* It's too much effort to get tickets to fly to Las Vegas. It's too much effort to put your golf clubs in the car. You just don't have the energy or the enthusiasm you once had.

Spending trends tend to follow this progression as well. You'll probably spend more in the earlier years of retirement than the later years. However, even though you are spending less money on activities during the no-go years, you may have to spend more on health care—as much as 20 percent of the budget for some people.

Because of this spending trend from early to late retirement, the younger you are, the more stocks you will typically have in your

Keep in mind that there is no assurance that any strategy will ultimately be successful or profitable nor protect against a loss.

portfolio. The stock-to-bond ratio tends to change with the decades because of risk. Stocks are inherently riskier and have a more variable rate of return than bonds do. As you get older, you generally want a steadier income stream from bonds, as opposed to a variable income stream from stocks.

You might have a fifty-fifty stock to bond allocation when you first retire. Toward the end of retirement you might have 70 percent bonds and 30 percent stocks. Again, like everything in your retirement plan, the allocation of your nest egg in stocks versus bonds will vary not only according to your age but also your tolerance for risk. The plan is completely personalized for *you*.

YOUR RETIREMENT INCOME STRATEGY

Based on my discussion with you during our discovery meeting, my team and I will draw on current market research and our own professional experience to create a personalized plan.

Your portfolio will include a combination of investment types designed to help you work toward your goals and tailored to how far away from retirement you are.

A week or two after our discovery session, I will ask you to return to my office to learn about your retirement-income strategy. We'll talk about when it would be appropriate for you (or your spouse) to start Social Security and when your pension should kick in. We'll talk about the size of the monthly paycheck you can expect to receive according to your assets. If you are not yet eligible for Medicare, we'll discuss health care and how to fund it. If there will be a gap before Social Security, we'll talk about how your nest egg can generate income during that time.

I will show you what you might receive every month in Income Today with a statement like the one below.

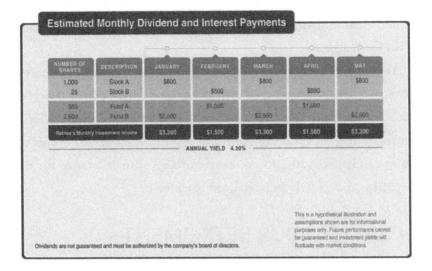

I'll also show you a visualization of your individual plan, like this one, that includes Income Today, Income Tomorrow, and Flexibility Dollars. I'll encourage you to take as much time as you need and to ask as many questions as you'd like. I won't implement your plan until you feel that you understand it completely.

At this point in the process, I find that about 15–20 percent of people want to make an adjustment here and there to their plan. As long as you fully understand the ramifications of making a change, that is fine. What I try to avoid is having people leave the office with questions. I want you to feel empowered to go into your retirement, confident that your money will be there to support your needs and goals.

IMPLEMENTING AND MANAGING YOUR PLAN

With your consent, then, we will complete the necessary purchases to launch your investment plan, putting your money to work for you. Then my team and I will continually monitor your portfolio and consult with you on a regular basis. As your circumstances change and the markets fluctuate, we will discuss investment alternatives and adapt your plan as needed.

In addition we will meet on a regular basis to discuss how the plan is working for you. Do you need more to live on? Are you ill and need more health-care dollars? Do we need to change beneficiaries? We may talk more when you first set up the plan than years into retirement when you are very familiar with it.

Keep in mind that there is no assurance that any strategy will ultimately be successful or profitable nor protect against a loss.

QUESTION AND ANSWER

What can I learn at the Social Security website?

The Social Security website (found at ssa.gov) is a wealth of information. A visitor to the site can sign up for a "mySocialSecurity" account and view his or her benefits at various ages. You can sign up to initiate benefits (for Social Security, disability, or Medicare). There are retirement estimators and financial calculators. This is a good place to get personalized information on your past employment wages, benefit eligibility at different ages, spouse or divorce benefits, and many other community resources.

How do I find any accounts that I might have left behind somewhere?

Every US state has an unclaimed-property program. Also known as "abandoned property," it typically came from accounts at financial institutions that haven't had any activity in over one year. (Returned mail to the companies from the USPS or closed email accounts are two ways that companies use to establish inactivity.) These assets are commonly uncashed dividend checks, refunds, tuition reimbursements, life insurance proceeds, security deposits, and contents from safe deposit boxes. Start your search by going to the various state websites and entering "unclaimed property." This search will need to be done for each state of past residence.

What tips do you have for finding an appropriate advisor for me?

Most clients will ask for referrals from friends, family, accountants, or attorneys. This is a good start. I would then look for credentials, which indicate that the advisor has kept current with changes in the industry. Both the CERTIFIED FINANCIAL PLANNER™ (CFP®) and CFA® (Chartered Financial Analyst™) certifications require significant levels of knowledge. Additionally, the FPA (Financial Planning Association) website can be searched by location and specialty. Take the time to generate a list of questions for the advisor. (E.g., how do you make recommendations, get paid, contact clients, evaluate stocks? Whatever it is that you want to understand.) Finally, make sure that you're comfortable with the advisor's style of explanation (using analogies, data, acronyms, etc.). Communication is essential, and it works best when the advisor and client are "speaking the same language."

CONCLUSION

Financial concepts and products will continue to evolve in order to meet the demands of retirees and retirement-income planning. Researchers will continue to find alternative approaches and make them available to the next generation of retirees, offering more choices—and more potential pitfalls.

The Piece by Piece™ model is designed to offer a commonsense approach to what can be a challenging emotional and financial transition into retirement. The value of your portfolio may fluctuate—and it's important to sell your "hens" at the right time—but in the meantime, our hens' egg production is designed to be sustained and utilized for years in the same way that a retirement portfolio can generate income for you. It becomes the foundation for our plan by striving to provide Income Today. The smaller percentages of the Piece by Piece™ model allocated to Income Tomorrow and Flexibility Dollars allow potential growth for future needs as well as unexpected occurrences.

Hopefully, the more you are able to understand how the pieces of your retirement income can provide for your future, the sooner you will start tuning out the continuous noise of media information and putting your Piece by Piece™ plan into place. It's never too soon to start.

Keep in mind that there is no assurance that any strategy will ultimately be successful or profitable nor protect against a loss.

Offices in Traverse City and Alden Michigan
231-331-5500
www.craigwealthadvisors.com

ABOUT THE AUTHOR

D ebbie grew up in a family business and started answering their phones at age seven during the regular reception- ist's disability. While in high school, Debbie moved on to the accounting department at *The Detroit News*. Her undergraduate degree is in economics from Kalamazoo College, and she spent her junior year at the International Institute in Madrid, Spain, where all class instruction was in Spanish. Following K-College graduation, she began a fifteen-year career at General Motors, which was spent mostly on the financial staff. This included serving as manager of Oldsmobile's $4.3 billion capital-management department.

Debbie has been passionately helping people plan for retirement since the 1990s. She began by taking an MBA from Northwestern University's Kellogg School of Management, and then she became a CERTIFIED FINANCIAL PLANNER™ professional. The CFP® program involved two to three years of study, ten to fifteen hours a week, to learn to apply financial-planning knowledge to real-life situations. The program culminated in a two-day, sixteen-hour exam covering the financial-planning process, tax planning, employee benefits and retirement planning, estate planning, and investment management and insurance. To earn the right to use the CFP® certi- fication trademarks, one then has to work in financial planning for several years and demonstrate proficiency.

The CFP® also has ethical standards—*Standards of Professional Conduct*—that "require CFP® professionals to put [their clients'] interests ahead of their own at all times and to provide their financial- planning services as a 'fiduciary'—acting in the best interest of their financial-planning clients. CFP° professionals are subject to CFP° Board sanctions if they violate these standards." More information about this designation is available at www.cfp.net.

Debbie continually improves her education, gets recertifications, and continues to learn—because the industry changes so much and so quickly. And keeping on top of her game becomes even more important as the industry changes and more people need to generate a monthly check in retirement because they do not have a pension or enough Social Security. To that end, she is, as of this writing, studying to be certified as a Retirement Income Certified Professional™ (RICP°) through a three-semester class that focuses on the principles of generating retirement income. She is also a CRPS°, or Chartered Retirement Plans Specialist™. This certification includes continuing education and renewal every two years to ensure that she stays on top of the new laws regarding retirement plans.